Praise for
White Lives Matter Most

If we want a world free of colonialism, one that could be more just, healthier, and environmentally protected, we need a new internationalism. We know that even when a colonized nation gains its independence, the nefarious and deleterious vestiges of colonialism continue affecting its citizens. Because they haven't been able to transcend their colonized mindset, the colonizer or colonizing nation takes advantage of this reality and transforms the former colony into a neocolony, thus perpetuating colonialism and continuing the exploitation of its former colony. Only with a new internationalism, free of colonies and of exploitation and oppression by the imperialist nations, can we hope to live in a world free of wars and in harmony with each other and with the environment. We must dare to make our planet a place where everything that makes life possible is protected and where the human race lives in harmony, peace, good health, and happiness. Lifelong solidarity organizer Matt Meyer's new book helps us—*dares us*—to move in this direction.

—Oscar López Rivera, Puerto Rican national hero, human
   rights organizer, and former political prisoner

In this provocative call to action, Matt Meyer asks that we rise to the challenge of our moment. He offers a beacon not a blueprint: a light onto the urgency of doing all we can to undermine empire and the racism on which it stands.

—Dan Berger, associate professor of Comparative Ethnic
   Studies at the University of Washington, author of *Captive
   Native: Black Prison Organizing in the Civil Rights Era*

This book is a call to move our antiracist politics off Twitter and into spaces of real comradeship and struggle. Meyer draws on the lessons of the civil rights, anti-war, and Black Power movements—specifically around questions of white solidarity and nonviolence—not for absolutist instructions but to bring strategy and nuance to current organizing. Meyer encourages us to move from identity politics to radical politics that can end white supremacy with accountability, inclusion, and love.

—Francesca Fiorentini, journalist, comedian, and producer and host of Al Jazeera Media Network's *Newsbroke* and the National Geographic Channel's *Explorer*

With passion and depth, Matt Meyer has led a fully engaged life as a white antiracist for decades as an educator, author, activist, and organizer. No matter how much you know about opposing racism, you, like I, will learn a tremendous amount about analyzing white supremacy, building our struggle against it, and reclaiming the humanity of all of us by reading this book.

—David Gilbert, anti-imperialist political prisoner, author of *Love and Struggle: My Life in SDS, the Weather Underground, and Beyond*

Longtime organizer and academic Matt Meyer adds new insights to the challenges and potential for white people in multiracial left movements. A key read for a deep understanding of lessons and mistakes from the past—and how leaders from these movements and all of us are learning from Black Lives Matter, immigrant rights movements, and the current fight against white supremacy.

—Dara Silverman, founding director of Showing Up for Racial Justice (SURJ) and former executive director of Jews for Racial and Economic Justice

WHITE LIVES MATTER MOST
And Other "Little" White Lies

MATT MEYER
Foreword by SONIA SANCHEZ

White Lives Matter Most and Other "Little" White Lies
Matt Meyer

© Matt Meyer 2019
This edition © PM Press 2019

PM Press
PO Box 23912
Oakland, CA 94623
www.pmpress.org

Cover design by John Yates/stealworks.com
Layout by Jonathan Rowland

ISBN: 978-1-62963-540-8
Library of Congress Control Number: 2018931518

10 9 8 7 6 5 4 3 2 1

Contents

Acknowledgments   ix

Forward: Organize   xi
Sonia Sanchez

Little White Lives   1

America Has *Always* Meant White Lives Matter Most   4

If Mental Illness Is the Problem, America Is Mentally Ill   13
Matt Meyer, David Ragland, and Natalie Jeffers

Refusing to Choose between Martin and Malcolm: 17
   Ferguson, Black Lives Matter, and a New Nonviolent
   Revolution
Matt Meyer, David Ragland, and Natalie Jeffers

Toward a Maroon Society: Working Together to Build   26
   a New World
Fred Ho, with Matt Meyer

Strategic Alliance Building: A Change Is Gonna Come   41

Redefining Revolution and Nonviolence: Reimagining   48
   Solidarity across Race, Class, Gender, and Generations

Oscar López Rivera: America's Mandela and His   52
   Movement Face the Future
Ana López and Matt Meyer

From Charlottesville to North Korea, White Supremacy   **67**
   Feeds Endless War

Extreme Solidarity   **71**

Looking at the White Left Historically   **77**

Conclusion: Removing Our White-Colored Glasses—   **91**
   Facing Reality and Fighting against Empire

About the Authors   **99**

Index   **104**

Acknowledgments

IN ADDITION TO ALL MY COAUTHORS, THIS BOOK WOULD not even have been conceptually possible without the mentorship of Mawaina Sowa Kouyate, Papa Bill Sutherland, and Luis Nieves Falcón. From conception to implementation, my practice has been shaped and matured through decades of struggle within the War Resisters League, with special memories of my brother Jon Cohen, and through the comradeship of Resistance in Brooklyn. Constant and current central committee leadership comes, as ever, from Meg Starr, Michael Meyer-Starr, Molly Soo Meyer-Starr, and Elspeth Nene Meyer. They are my harshest critics, my most beloved community. Craig O'Hara of PM Press has had a gentle touch, an encouraging voice, and a wise balance between business and family that makes radical possibilities within the U.S. empire seem just a bit less impossible; his and my PM colleagues Ramsey, Jonathan, Steven, Michael, and so many others help remind and reassure me through their words and incredibly stalwart work that writing and reading are still worthwhile pursuits. Poet, copyeditor, and organizer Steve Bloom of the Old and New Project has been a steady and thoughtful contributor to my thinking. Finally, from the idea to the final page, comrade, friend, and copyeditor extraordinaire Betsy Mickel whipped this manuscript into shape.

FORWARD: ORGANIZE

SONIA SANCHEZ

Matt Meyer poignantly points out that
America *has* Always Meant White Lives Matter Most.

And Matt, along with Oscar Lopez Rivera and Ana Lopez,
with Fred Ho,
and with Natalie Jeffers, and David Ragland's Ferguson Truth
Tellers
Tell us
that it will never change
unless we organize.
Decolonize our minds.
Organize.
Wipe out white supremacy.
Organize.
Put an end to patriarchy,
Racism,
Greed,
Wars,
Poverty,
and ignorance.
Unless we
Organize.
Organize.
Organize.

Poet-protester-prophet extraordinaire Sonia Sanchez, in her commencement address to the Swarthmore College Class of 2018, challenged the young leaders in this way: "You my brothers, my sisters, must finally answer the most important question of the twenty-first century: What does it mean to be human?" In Sister Sonia's contribution to this book, she agreed that we reprint this older reflection, "An Anthem (for the ANC and Brandywine Peace Community)," previously published in *Under a Soprano Sky* (Africa World Press, 1987) and *Shake Loose My Skin* (Beacon, 1999).

An Anthem
(for the ANC and Brandywine Peace Community)

Our vision is our voice
we cut through the country
where madmen goosestep in tune to Guernica.

we are people made of fire
we walk with ceremonial breaths
we have condemned talking mouths.

we run without legs
we see without eyes
loud laughter breaks over our heads.

give me courage so I can spread
it over my face and mouth.

we are secret rivers
with shaking hips and crests
come awake in our thunder
so that our eyes can see behind trees.

for the world is split wide open
and you hide your hands behind your backs
for the world is broken into little pieces
and you beg with tin cups for life.

are we not more than hunger and music?
are we not more than harlequins and horns?
are we not more than color and drums?
are we not more than anger and dance?

give me courage so I can spread it
over my face and mouth.

we are the shakers
walking from top to bottom in a day
we are like Shango
involving ourselves in acts
that bring life to the middle
of our stomachs.

we are coming towards you madmen
shredding your death talk
standing in front with mornings around our waist
we have inherited our prayers from the rain
our eyes from the children of Soweto.

red rain pours over the land
and our fire mixes with the water.

give me courage so I can spread
it over my face and mouth.

LITTLE WHITE LIVES

THE TITLE OF THIS BOOK IS INTENDED TO PROVOKE.

Its simple assertion is neither original nor fully my own. It is an observation that any progressive person living in or observant of the empire we call America should assume, almost a priori, when thinking about the USA. That we don't take action based on this assumption—that we can still be surprised, challenged, or even offended by the idea that maybe Black lives should matter, too—is one of the monumental problems facing our twenty-first-century times.

That we can't all agree that the USA has always meant (and continues to mean) "white lives matter most" is the great, big "little white lie" at the center of our little white lives.

Recognizing the truth of that fact, becoming truth-tellers about the way we value some lives and invalidate others, is the urgent task of this era. But it is not a new task. And it is not simply about race.

I recently returned from the Howard Zinn Book Fair, where the latest of my anthologies received a special spotlight. *Look for Me in the Whirlwind: From the Panther 21 to 21st-Century Revolutions*, which I coedited with my New York City–based teaching colleague dequi kioni-sadiki and coauthored with original members of the New York Black Panther Party Sekou Odinga, Dhoruba Bin Wahad, Jamal Joseph, Shaba Om, Sundiata Acoli, and others, was called "more relevant than ever" in a starred review from *Publishers Weekly*. This is high praise for a history book, especially when coming from such a mainstream source. Zinn, the preeminent radical historian of the last century, became an iconic figure based primarily on his *People's History of the United States*, which is used extensively in high school and college classrooms across the continent. But when I challenged the engaged and already conscious group of attendees at our session at the book fair to name the title of the work that most cogently reflected on white lives and race in U.S. history, no hands went up.

So many know *A People's History of the United States* (or Howard Zinn's version of it). Yet few have even heard of J. Sakai's *Settlers: The Mythology of the White Proletariat from Mayflower to Modern*, the stunning work that meticulously charts the growth of the U.S. economy and political organization through the essential lens of race. It is not so much that everything in *Settlers* is correct or holds true for all time; many critics, including Sakai himself, have written eloquently on the complicated confluence of race and class. The point is, even as another generation comes to terms with the inequity and inequalities of our times, the major intellectual work of the past generation looking to break this cycle has hardly even been considered.

I've worked my entire adult life as an educator, and at no point have I felt more frustrated about the idea that education—at this moment—will hardly be enough. Now is a time for action.

The last school I worked at was named after arguably the greatest mind produced in the U.S. during the last century. W.E.B. Du Bois was not merely a profound educator and author, he is widely recognized as the founder of modern sociology. He was also, of course, one of the founders of the oldest ongoing civil rights organizations in the country, the

National Association for the Advancement of Colored People (NAACP), and considered himself a socialist, communist, and Pan-Africanist. As the first African American to earn a doctorate from Harvard University, he was aware at an early age of the power of words and pronouncements—but had no problem prophetically asserting in 1903 that the greatest challenge of the twentieth century would be "the color line."

More than one hundred years later, Du Bois seems more correct today than ever.

More than one hundred years later, the top Department of Education administrators assigned to the school had little or no idea in whose hallways they were working, regularly referring to it as "the web school," as if named after some studious spider.

Our little white lives continue to take up spaces we barely know exist.

America Has *Always* Meant White Lives Matter Most

Most conscientious people in the U.S. today know that Black Lives Matter—or the Movement for Black Lives—may have started out as a Twitter hashtag but has grown into something much greater than that. Whether or not, in the era of Donald Trump, it has reached anything close to the potential some have seen for it is a matter of debate, both within and outside of the Black community. On the one hand, some elders of the Black liberation movement suggest that the upsurge of activities following the Ferguson, Missouri, police murder of Michael Brown and the many reports of deaths at the hands of law enforcement since have still not coalesced into something worthy of the moniker "movement." On the other hand, racist constructions—like the slogan "Blue Lives Matter," which flaunted police power in an age of unprecedented police militarization—set back the conversations substantially.

In the interest of creating space for genuine dialogue across the generations, political tendencies, and geographic distance, a private retreat was organized in Amherst, Massachusetts, in the spring of 2016, bringing together many grassroots Black Lives Matter organizers and a few key founders of the sixties era Student Nonviolent Coordinating Committee (SNCC), the Black Panther Party, and others. Out of forty or so participants, a small handful of "white folks"—from the new group Showing Up for Racial Justice (SURJ) and the San Francisco–based Catalyst Project, who have become known for their annual organizer trainings held in the name of white civil rights icon Anne Braden—were also included, mainly to serve as supportive listeners. Young folks from the Dream Defenders of Florida, from the Justice League of New York (one of whom went on to co-coordinate the massive Women's March at the time of Trump's inauguration), and many others came out for the frank conversation. Though little known because the gathering was more about internal relationship / alliance building and long-term strategy than about self-aggrandizing publicity or statements of intent, the Amherst gathering served an important intermediary goal of looking at how best to build broad unity in disjointed times. More work along these lines must surely be done.

As part of the weekend of private conversations, one public event was held for the students, staff, and community of Western Massachusetts. This region, after all, was the base for many SNCC workers, and the University of Massachusetts / Amherst—whose W.E.B. Du Bois Library (holding most of Du Bois's papers) is the tallest academic research library in the world—was home to James Baldwin, Julius Lester, and many others. The event included presentations from Ferguson's passionate Rev. Osagyefo Sekou, from Cal State's Pan-African Studies chair Melina Abdullah, and from yours truly—representing a "white ally" point of view.

Black feminist icon Dr. Gloria Joseph, in Amherst in part to promote *The Wind Is Spirit: The Life, Love, and Legacy of Audre Lorde* (chronicling Joseph's and Lorde's lifelong partnership), paid me the highest compliment at the close of my talk. "Matt, you need to get that published!" she exclaimed. It appears here for the first time.

Over Easter weekend in Raleigh, North Carolina, in 1960, Ella Baker helped bring together some student leaders and some movement elders, and the Student Nonviolent Coordinating Committee (SNCC) was born. Just six years later—after both dramatic defeats and astonishing victories—several key leaders of SNCC's Atlanta Project put out a position paper that, to this very day, remains little read and even less understood. When, in 1966, Stokely Carmichael (later known as Kwame Ture) took over as chair of the organization and popularized the call for Black Power, the die was cast for a myth that has confused movements for decades since.

If we are to truly build more effective movements of the future, we must move beyond the myths of the past.

The first and biggest myth is about white people.

Essentially, the mistaken story goes, SNCC and Stokely kicked out all of the white people in a separatist move that split the movement. The truth is, as whites flooded the offices and membership of the main national Black youth group, a critique developed—based on the principles of self-determination and on an analysis of what SNCC needed to do to more effectively build within the Black community. Whatever good work individual white folks did and whatever deep friendships developed across the color line, several basic organizational problems remained, and the Atlanta Project position paper articulated the problems brought about by a fully integrated infrastructure:

- Attitudes of superiority or paternalism that whites consciously or unconsciously bring to Black communities;

- the unwillingness of whites to deal with the roots of racism that lie within the white community; and the fact that
- whites, though sometimes liberal (or even radical) on an individual level, are *still* collective symbols of oppression to many in the Black community—due to the collective power that whites have over Black *lives*.

A solution seemed clear: allow and empower the Black student leaders to have full control over SNCC and press for supportive white allies to do the also necessary and not easy work of dealing with the roots of racism that lie within the white community. Whites would continue the vital work of dealing with the white supremacist and paternalistic realities that existed at all levels of society and could work alongside (but not always or primarily within) the same groups as Black comrades, colleagues, and friends.

In coalitions, united fronts, and strategic campaign spaces, folks could always come together for mutual aid and solidarity. But not every group at every moment of its life would work as if being mixed or multiracial was the *only* way to move forward for social change.

Today, fifty years after the call for Black Power, fifty years since SNCC's Atlanta Project set down this challenge for whites seeking to be antiracist, many of us sadly believe that—for the most part—white progressives and radicals *still* Have Not Been Moved to tackle white supremacy head on.

Anyone, Black or white, who ever met Kwame Ture knew that his basic call for *all* people—his greatest lesson and most consistent talking point—was that *before* one could begin to discuss building united fronts and coalitions (and Kwame was a great believer in coalition work), one must do "three" essential things at whatever level one was able: organize, organize, and organize!

It could be in a local church subcommittee or on the central committee of a grand vanguard party; it could be in a regional self-defense association or in a national secular nonviolence group. But wherever one was, whatever else was happening in one's life, no positive change could ever take place—no unified campaign could ever be successful—if we weren't working within an organizational framework and if we weren't working to build our organizations.

This leads me to a second myth that is often the cause for debate and division. There are those who argue that it is clear that armed struggle didn't work or could never work in the U.S.; others argue just as vehemently that nonviolence has been an utter failure, resulting in liberalism and passive movements without teeth. In fact, however, we've seen pacifists and Panthers strategizing together, with many saying that it is time we refuse to choose between the legacy of Martin or of Malcolm—that those two men and the movements they led may have had many differences, but they also had many points of convergence: *both* were becoming increasingly internationalist; *both* were concerned with the connections between economic and racial issues.

We do not now have to repeat the fights of past generations; we *do* have to resist the absolutist arguments that some white folks make about not getting too militant, too rowdy, too Black, too strong—and remind those folks that being militant is not the same as being militaristic, that being confrontational is not the same as being violent.

We must be *more* militant, more creatively confrontational, and our only absolute must be that we will *not* become absolutists, not inflexible ideologues for any notion that suggests that there is only one correct way to build for radical change.

Finally, we must move beyond the myth about what the U.S. is and what it can be. It may be true that some reforms are both good and necessary in the struggles against racist police violence and mass incarceration. It may be true that we must fight the good fight to push back the vicious privatization of education, health care, and community services that make clear that the U.S. is not committed to democracy or justice for all.

But it is surely also true that America is doing more than simply locking up people of African descent at a rate reminiscent of apartheid South Africa; America is doing more than warehousing political prisoners—especially from the Black liberation movement, Black Panthers, and others—for thirty, forty, fifty-plus years of torture behind bars. If we understand that racism is a combination of prejudice plus power and that power comes from concrete structural sources, most especially land and capital, then we must face the institutional realities of white supremacy well beyond interpersonal dynamics.

It is clear that if we are to examine the history of the U.S. from before 1776 till today, from South to North and Hawaii to Puerto Rico, from occupied Mexico to what some call New Afrika, if we are to look at the U.S. less as a nation and more as an empire—an imperial power in deep economic decline—if we are to look sharply at the empire we live in, we cannot help but conclude that the United States of America is a prison house of nations.

That is why it has been so hard to move beyond the historic calls for new ways to engage in struggle.

That is why, when the cry "Black Lives Matter" is proclaimed, so often we hear the confused retort, "But don't all lives matter?"

To this we must simply and clearly say:

- America has always meant White Lives Matter Most.
- From the genocidal policies of the Middle Passage and Manifest Destiny, America has always meant White Lives Matter Most.
- From the days of Jim Crow lynching to the police-Klan realities of "blue cap by day, white hood by night," America has always meant White Lives Matter Most.
- When we learn *today* that some prisons in the Deep South are being built at a rate directly proportional to the low test scores obtained in predominantly Black public schools in standardized tests administered to third and fourth graders, we know that America *still means* White Lives Matter Most.
- America has always meant White Lives Matter Most.

Black Lives Matter must mean an end to the entire institution of white supremacy and thus an end to the U.S. empire as well.

So what are we to do?

The lessons are in a history without myths.

***

Recently, some white organizers have begun to once again take up the call for rigorous work in white communities. We have white organizers who are working to Show Up for Racial Justice and more, from the simple act of putting a sign on your lawn (for those who can afford lawns and whose houses won't be burned down when displaying such a sign), to beginning grassroots neighborhood conversations about why we still must assert that Black Lives Matter in a post-Obama era. There are white activists who are struggling to be catalysts for radical change, training organizers in the tradition of Anne Braden and working to understand that only a successful Black liberation movement will mean collective liberation for all.

And we have organizers who are looking to the examples of Marilyn Buck and David Gilbert, self-criticisms and all, who proudly worked with the likes of Black Liberation Army combatant Sekou Odinga (out of prison after more than thirty-three years behind bars as an unacknowledged U.S. political prisoner) and with many other Black Panther leaders who still languish in U.S. prisons. Some of those folks established organizations that worked directly and structurally under the leadership and control of organizations within the Black liberation movement. There are some organizers who understand what Minister Malcolm X meant when he said that "if we want some white allies, we need the kind like Old John Brown." Who understand that behind the scenes, Captain Brown, who took his leadership directly from General Harriet Tubman, received a lot of financial and logistical support from the Quakers of his day.

We must ask ourselves:

- When most police department headquarters that house racist officers are geographically situated within white communities, and
- when so many white progressives suggest concern about violence and racism and wrongdoing,

- *why* are there not more marches within these communities to shut these police departments *down*?

We have many questions to ask and much work still to do. When we organize even in the most determined of solidarities, we will make mistakes. But as a wise comrade, Clare Bayard of the Catalyst Project, reminded me, it is time for white folks to get more comfortable about being uncomfortable.

We must get comfortable with the discomfort of not being at the center or the head of all things.

We must get comfortable with the discomfort of not being in control of the funds.

We must get comfortable with the discomfort of not being in control of the agenda.

We must get comfortable with the discomfort of not turning away when the focus is elsewhere, the tide is low, and it seems that all is lost.

Together, we are now at a high-tide moment when movements can collide, but they can also come together—and they must.

Now is a time when *mass resistance* is possible and happening, when coalitions and united fronts are ripe for the building, when we *can* be moved to more effective campaigns and *can* move together toward more principled unity.

Together we *can*; together we *must*. Freedom and liberation for all!

IF MENTAL ILLNESS IS THE PROBLEM, AMERICA IS MENTALLY ILL

MATT MEYER, DAVID RAGLAND, AND NATALIE JEFFERS

This piece and the one that follows helped lay the basis for the Amherst retreat. They are presented here with permission, having been previously published online in Counterpunch *in early 2016. They were used as part of the Movement for Black Lives "Reclaim MLK Day" push—to energize the annual celebrations of the birth of Dr. Martin Luther King, Jr. with local, action-based initiatives worthy of the man himself.*

THE YEAR 2015 WAS ONE OF EXCEPTIONALLY OVERT POLICE violence against Black folks and of tragic mass shootings. A common response to these events has been that they are the result of "sick" individuals. Many conservatives have suggested that the shooters were mentally ill: that the problem was a proliferation of bad people not a proliferation of guns. When, however, the murderers happen to be people "of color," the narrative often changes to one of terrorism and extremism (though the NRA position remains consistently progun, even defending the rights of the San Bernardino terrorists to acquire their weaponry).

In fact, according to the U.S. Department of Health and Human Services, just 3 to 5 percent of violent acts are attributable to mental illness. In fact, police have frequently simply treated nonviolent mental illness as a capital offense requiring instant lethal force.

But what about inciting people to violence? We should not fail to recognize the systemic interplay between race, class, NRA lobbying, and gun-related deaths. The myth of Black criminality is conveniently used to replace an institutional analysis of what is wrong with our country. These myths, both for police and for the majority of Americans, justify summary executions, the refusal of police to acknowledge the wrongdoings of fellow officers, and the courts' general unwillingness to hold individual officers accountable, opting instead to prop up a system of cover-up, delay, and denial. The rare exceptions boldly highlight the rule.

America is literally violently ill. This society is feverish on the valorization of violence. Victims of violence—speaking out and demanding accountability for racism (as in Charleston or Ferguson) or regarding violent sexism (as in Planned Parenthood)—are blamed as the cause. This "blame culture" is a symptom of America's frankly sick relationship to violence.

In order for healing to occur, we must trace our disease back to its sources, which include the fact that the slave-owning colonies that revolted against the British created a "democracy" for whites only. Since America's founding, whites have used widespread violence against Blacks, Indigenous populations, and women to gain free labor and land. Civil rights law professor Michelle Alexander chronicles aspects of the continuous repression of Black folks, from Reconstruction era violence to our current prison system, which disproportionately incarcerates Blacks and Latinos. It seems that our denial of the past leads us to denial of the present crisis.

Without facing our shared history frankly, including greater attempts to make amends, we cannot expect anything different from our future. To be clear, the authors do not support any violence. Having said that, history shows that, for example, Black Panthers who invoked their Second Amendment right to bear arms faced extraordinary, illegal, state-sponsored repression, while armed white vigilantes were allowed to carry assault weapons at Ferguson protests. Why the double standard? Is it possible that guns in public places are *always* in the wrong hands?

It is no coincidence that this year of violence and fear was also marked by a huge increase in gun sales, stoked by politicians who suggest that survival of the American status quo is dependent on being armed against Black, brown, immigrant, Muslim, and other "categories" that engender fear in impressionable white Americans. Yes, caution is important, but if we went by the statistics, perhaps we would disband all sports or emasculate all men—they are the rapists and molesters of little girls, after all. But in America, we value each individual—we don't judge people by the "race," religion, class, or other category into which they were born.

While many Americans try to protect some tiny bit of existential comfort gained in part from injustice, countless others are humiliated, discriminated against, jailed, and killed through violent policing and the consequences of being born the wrong race and class. We are all, however, born into a systemic culture of silence and denial, trained to overlook how—from the beginning—militarization has mixed with money and racial matters to build this world-class empire.

America is ill, and the cause is the ingrained violence that comes from racism, materialism, sexism, economic injustice, and beyond. We must, as a nation, cure this illness before it becomes terminal. In Dr. Martin Luther King, Jr.'s 1967 speech, he urged that America needed "a radical revolution of values"—exhorting us to move toward a "person-oriented" society rather than being "thing-oriented." The radical truth-telling coming from Ferguson offers a remedy for the rest of this nation. Transparency, accountability, and confronting the powers that be (and our own neighbors as well when needed) is, as intercultural communications scholar Imani Michelle Scott suggests, our only real hope for peaceful survival.

At this moment in history, we must ask ourselves: What kind of nation are we to become? Will we continue to choose money and profit instead of the lives of many of its citizens? When we are told that it is "reasonable" to shoot and kill a twelve-year-old child like Tamir Rice, who was holding a toy gun in a park, when we face a consistent string of non-indictments of police officers engaged in racially motivated violence, when Congress refuses to end the ban on research of mass shootings, it seems that a resounding "yes" is our sad answer.

If we cannot and do not speak the truth about today's crimes against humanity, the U.S. will not begin the long and much-needed march toward recovery, healing, and true democracy. May this year open our hearts to the best of who we are and can be together.

REFUSING TO CHOOSE BETWEEN MARTIN AND MALCOLM

FERGUSON, BLACK LIVES MATTER, AND A NEW NONVIOLENT REVOLUTION

MATT MEYER, DAVID RAGLAND, AND NATALIE JEFFERS

THE TRIPLE-THREAT CRISIS OF RACISM, MILITARISM, AND materialism continues to define the American empire: unprecedented levels of racially biased incarceration, increasingly disempowering and divided educational systems based on race and class, and statistics that show that Blacks are nine times more likely to be killed by police. Despite a president (in an extraordinary act of self-denial) proclaiming in his final major address that there is no Black America, the evidence suggests that we are living in a particularly dangerous time, especially if you are or know a young person of African descent.

The year 2015 was not only one of fear, brutality, and injustice, it was a year of sustained resistance that honored not only a strong national Black radical politics of organizing, but also helped cultivate a new and thriving, nonviolent international movement for Black liberation. As we enter 2016, the Movement for Black Lives must navigate in uncharted territory and hazardous spaces, accompanied by a vigorous knowledge of self, a thriving and committed community of activists and organizers who are cognizant of the need for guiding principles, and the creation of a Black radical national policy platform.

The movement is malleable—to be shaped and reshaped depending on the needs of both specific moments and long-term, community-based goals. At the core will remain three essential demands: divestment from racist systems and investment in Black communities; community self-control and community-centered decision-making; and the creation of alternative institutions and radical spaces that express and reflect one's right to live freely. These principles are inspired by a reimagination of what it means to build radical democracy laid down by a generation of youth organizers like Martin Luther King, Jr. and Malcolm X, Ella Baker and Fannie Lou Hamer, Kwame Ture and Angela Davis, and so many others.

It is fitting that on Dr. King's birthday weekend in 2016, an intergenerational, intersectional movement of Black radicals and their allies are collectively organizing to reclaim the moment, using MLK's tools of nonviolent civil disobedience and direct action to launch a "Year of Resistance and Resilience." Coordinated actions taken across the U.S. and the world will ensure that this birthday weekend is understood as a time for visible resistance to current injustices not simply celebratory affirmations of past victories.

Building an Affirmation

Black Lives Matter is an ideological and political intervention in a world where Black lives are systematically and intentionally targeted for demise. It is an affirmation of Black folks as human and an affirmation of our contributions to society, humanity, resilience, and resistance in the face of deadly oppression.

At the root of this movement is a critique of violence. At times this past year, it seemed that the empire commonly known as the USA has rarely been so divided. Alongside the social divisions, however, it seems that the rising new movements may, at last, be in the process of uniting different struggles working across the many landscapes of oppression and uniting philosophical approaches too often used to divide us.

The current movement emerging from the Ferguson uprising, Black Lives Matter and other Black liberation formations, has learned from the leader-focused movements of the past not to rely on single, charismatic, too-often-male leaders who centralize, mainstream, or silo organizational life, principles, or culture(s). Nevertheless, even though some youth organizers will say, "This ain't yo' daddy's Civil Rights Movement," the philosophical specter of past generations echoes through modern debates about strategy and tactics. These include real differences of style and preference, including the efficacy of reform versus radical demands, the power of mass civil resistance and nonviolence versus the legitimacy and need for armed self-defense, and the different roles that solidarity and alliance building can take. These differences, however, have too often been posited as do-or-die dichotomies, falsely suggesting that there is only one path to effective and lasting social change.

X vs. Jr.

The images of Rev. Martin Luther King, Jr. and Minister Malcolm X are rolled out by the movement and their critics in equal measure. They swiftly and elegantly deliver historical visions that slot conveniently into particular, not always accurate, not often useful historical narratives. One is the providence and revolutionary, the other is pacifist and reformist.

We are too often instructed to forget the intersections where their actions, movements, and messages meet, and there is good reason why we are distracted from connecting these dots: to connect is to find new meaning in cooperation and collaboration between organizing groups. Yet there is much evidence we can draw from that would bridge the gap between Martin and Malcolm, including one bright, smiling, brotherly moment captured when the two men met and shook hands across the divides of their times. That moment—with two men committed to both racial justice and human rights for all, committed to an internationalism that understood the U.S. empire and the struggle of Black folks in a global context, committed to an understanding that tactical differences should never stand in the way of principled unity—beckons us to a twenty-first-century imperative.

We must *refuse to choose* between Martin and Malcolm. This time is our time to reimagine and practice revolutionary nonviolence.

Rejecting and Accepting the Past

While rejecting the representation of two myopic heteronormative male narratives of liberation, Malcolm and Martin offer a recognizable context to begin a critical conversation about what our Black liberation past has inspired and what popular culture can diminish.

Scholarship and common sense have already laid down most of what we need to know. As each of those two giants engaged with the world outside the U.S. borders, they grew in understanding that the problem of the "Black" world within the U.S. could not be solved merely through U.S. legislative or political remedies or through a single ideological or tactical approach. They clearly understood that the reforms of their earlier days would not be sufficient in ridding the U.S. or the world of the white supremacy that lay at its very foundation;

a revolution—whether of values or of arms or of a combined social resistance—would be needed for true emancipation on a global, diasporic scale.

There is, of course, a dualism here that we shouldn't simply avoid: armed and nonviolent approaches suggest different types of tactical considerations with likely different results. Missing, though, in almost all past tactical debates but present in the Black Lives Matter movement is the creation of spaces that develop a revolutionary and militant nonviolence mindset and discipline, borne of highly organized mass civil disobedience and resistant direct actions to shut down and completely disrupt "business as usual," dismantle racist systems, and transform institutions through acts of self-determination and reparations.

Most historians agree that Malcolm and Martin were killed for beginning to make transnational, strategic, and philosophical connections, and that the FBI's Counterintelligence Program that hunted them both continues to this day, though with different names and in different forms. It continues to seek to "expose, disrupt, misdirect, discredit, or otherwise neutralize the activities" of all those struggling for Black liberation.

The U.S. national security state went to outright war against the Black Panthers, their allies, and others who came after, but the spirit of the Panthers marches strong in the minds and on the T-shirts of youth organizers bearing slogans like "Assata Taught Me." It is also in the present, intergenerational radical learning spaces created to facilitate dialogue with the elders of past struggles.

By anchoring to the traditions of Black radical politics, the movement builders of today refuse to perpetuate the continued assassination of Dr. King, burying him in a soft focused, nostalgic, and "dreamy" 1963. We refuse to end

King's story with "I Have a Dream," as if he never was a young radical who was imprisoned, beaten, and discredited, as if he never grew into a powerful movement leader defying many advisers and funders by speaking out sharply against the war in Vietnam and in favor of economic justice for all. We refuse to go along with state-sponsored attempts to bury Black radicals behind bars as U.S. political prisoners or in exile with bounties on their heads, and so we spotlight the words—sent from Cuba—of Black Liberation Army leader Assata Shakur. Her most recent writing implores us to remember that "this is the 21st century and we need to redefine r/evolution. this planet needs a people's r/evolution. a humanist r/evolution. r/evolution is not about bloodshed or about going to the mountains and fighting. . . . the fundamental goal of r/evolution must be peace. . . . r/evolution is love."

In August 1963, as hundreds of thousands were marching on Washington, DC, to assert that "jobs and freedom" were still necessary for the descendants of enslaved Africans one hundred years after the end of the Civil War, Martin declared that America had offered Black folks "a bad check," one marked "insufficient funds" in the areas of liberty and justice. On that day, when Malcolm was suggesting that the march itself was a sellout, a conscious person wanting to take action would have had to make a logistical choice: to go to DC or stay home. A few months later, in Malcolm's "Message to the Grassroots," he clarified his differences with the civil rights leadership and sharpened his own definition of revolution. "The Black revolution," he stated, "is worldwide in scope and in nature. The Black revolution is sweeping Asia, sweeping Africa, rearing its head in Latin America. . . . Revolution overturns and destroys everything that gets in its way. . . . Revolution is based on land."

More than fifty years since those thunderous messages, we no longer need to make a choice. The mainstream history textbooks would like to freeze-frame Martin in 1963, having his dream and nothing more. They would like to cut Malcolm out altogether or else freeze him in some internal extremist, Muslim-based, fratricidal debacle. Martin came closer to Malcolm in his concern for what might be described as reparations or redistribution of wealth. Malcolm's attempt to take the U.S. to the United Nations for its violation of human rights offers a glimpse into his strategic, peaceful, coalition thinking, similar to King's gathering of international support and cross-movement, interfaith work.

New Moments, Nuances, New Movements

Theologian James Cone taught us to look beyond the whitewashed images of Malcolm versus Martin. Student activist Ashoka Jegroo told us that today's movements need not dichotomize those men as opposing sentinels. Charles Cobb, Akinyele Umoja, Sally Bermanzohn, and others have provided detailed works showing the nuances involved in the real movements of the 1950s, '60s, and '70s, suggesting that today we can and must go beyond false dichotomies.

In 2016, we must do more than simply acknowledge that we need not choose between Martin and Malcolm. To be effective, we must actively engage in the texts of Baldwin and Fanon; Dellinger and Braden; Lee Boggs, Butler, and Lorde; as well as hooks and Abu-Jamal and West. We must learn from a diasporic history of resistance and rebellion, from Haiti, Trinidad, and Jamaica; Ghana, Guinea Bissau, and Mozambique; Chile, Costa Rica, and Brazil; India, East Timor, and Vietnam; and—yes—the streets of San Juan and Brixton. We must interweave, interconnect, and intersect nuanced arguments, achievements, and concerns and be willing to critique and challenge one another as we reimagine society and explore our universe for new suns.

There is much debate about what makes for effective and transformative movement building—on local, national, or transnational scales. This much at least, from the last half century, seems clear: a merger of ideological and technical thinking will be needed, along with full access to and (re)distribution of all natural, material, and human resources. A revolutionary nonviolent praxis will require:

- a combination of reform and more radical measures, leading up to fully transformative and lasting change;
- a multiplicity of intersectional strategies and tactics that expand what we consider as nonviolence;
- a disciplined understanding and preparation for the fact that casualties and bloodshed occur in all revolutions and that militarism on the part of revolutionaries is always a costly error;
- massive training for mass organizing between social, economic, political, and environmental movements, using imaginative, creative, resistance-oriented means;
- concrete, grassroots, constructive programs that seek to build new societies and alternative institutions and that invest in Black communities and the communities of other historically oppressed peoples and nations; and
- explicit programs to eradicate white supremacy and heteronormative patriarchy, with the goal of liberation for all people.

This is not to say that the U.S. today, despite the ebullient mood on some campuses, is—to use a favorite phrase of Kwame Ture (aka Stokely Carmichael)—"ready for revolution." It *is* to say that radicals across different struggles and movements today might do well to step carefully around the dividing lines of past decades. We must find intersections and opportunities that exist in these new spaces, building unity where our elders could not. As the U.S. empire shows growing signs of decline, lashing out and closing ranks at anything beyond the 1% ruling elite, opportunities for radical change—as well as for vicious backlash and repression—will emerge with growing frequency. Let us not allow our people's movements to be divided, co-opted, or conquered—especially not along historic fault lines so clearly set up to divide and conquer us.

Liberation educator Paulo Freire noted that "violence is the tool of the master," and feminist poet Audre Lorde reminded us, "You cannot dismantle the master's house with the master's tools." So, let us reimagine new ways to build a society where Black people can live freely and dream, and let's find, as Barbara Deming implored, "equilibrium" in our revolutionary process.

The hegemonic status quo constantly reequips to co-opt, capture, and destroy our dissent. Today's movements must not seek to be "brought into the fold." The fold can only hold a few, and we no longer want the morphine of acceptance. Let us speak Truth to Empire, like the people of Ferguson and like U.S. political prisoners have been trying to do. It is time to refuse to fight our grandparents' battles and refuse to be limited by unnecessary past choices and false dichotomies.

It is time to build power, unite, and win!

TOWARD A MAROON SOCIETY
WORKING TOGETHER TO BUILD A NEW WORLD
FRED HO, WITH MATT MEYER

When, in the last years of his life, Chinese American radical musician, author, and organizer Fred Ho sought to consolidate his artistic-political work, he founded the organization Scientific Soul Sessions (SSS), which worked to seamlessly incorporate cutting-edge music and urgent messages for building effective social change and victory. Ho understood that sometimes a small group of professional organizers—not so much a vanguard as a disciplined and effective cadre—is needed to cut through the mess of confusion surrounding us in the heart of empire and the "belly of the beast." In a few short years, SSS produced countless programs on a multitude of topics, helped found the group Ecosocialist Horizons that thrives to this day, and engaged in challenging dialogues around what it will take to make lasting, radical change in the USA. SSS was also at the heart of the national freedom campaign for Black Panther political prisoner Russell Maroon Shoatz that saw the production of a book of his insightful writings and ultimately won him release from over twenty years of torturous solitary confinement. As a majority oppressed nationality revolutionary formation that nonetheless included some white folks, SSS wrestled with the question of white membership and how best to engage in long-term, principled internal struggle. As a nonpublic member of SSS and a longtime comrade of Fred

Ho, I (very imperfectly, making lots of mistakes) helped discuss what "being a Maroon" might mean for white people—even as we experienced how pervasive, entrenched, and odious "whiteness" is and can be—even in self-conscious radical contexts.

This article was a collaboration between the two of us, penned in the course of those struggles. It was originally published in a modified form on the New Clear Vision website. Several web-based comments are included here, as they reflect some thoughtful responses to our polemic.

"ANTIRACIST WHITES" ARE AGAINST SOME OF THE RIGHT things, but what are they for? As we fight for a society of more than just tolerance and "equality" but for true justice and liberation, our goal is to escape the matrix of the current systems. Like the historic Maroons of the past and the contemporary political prisoner Russell Maroon Shoatz, who continues to resist from behind enemy lines, we must build for a Maroon militancy that fully rejects the shackles of the past as we build for a new tomorrow.

"Antiracist whites" may believe in color-blindness, but we know that this is an impossibility in American society. Any obfuscation based on the belief that a "postracial" society can be achieved simply by ignoring or eradicating the notion of "race" is fundamentally mistaken about the roots of racism and the function it serves: the social reproduction of assimilation (and therefore control) within the American Empire.

"Antiracist whites" don't necessarily challenge the fundamental presumption of assimilation and integration into the USA (the Empire). Rather, racism is a byproduct and an integral part of the very construction of the USA as an empire that occupies and controls a vast territorial land base that extends for several thousands of miles into the Pacific Ocean and a thousand miles northward from its Northwest.

"Antiracist whites" may believe in the illusion that "Americans" can be changed for the better. This deception about the nature of America—confusing some national pride with the reality of imperialism—ignores the basic design of the USA: domination over peoples and territories.

"Antiracist whites" are typical of the entire (white) left: willing to acknowledge some degree of "white skin privilege," willing to be berated by some megalomaniacal Third World leaders (of their choosing) without challenging them, willing to accept the inevitability that the left will be white majority controlled.

"Antiracist whites" may be content to serve as "race traitors"—special white folks who somehow transcend race because of their theoretical or academic views but fail to actually engage in constructing liberated territories or spaces (Maroon societies) that escape from the Empire.

"Antiracist whites" may be content to organize solely inside white communities out of a sense of obligation and political responsibility (to relieve whites of their racism), without questioning whether those whites need to or should dismember and destroy the territorial integrity of the Empire.

History has shown that these whites are unacceptable; they will more than likely show their "true colors" through Eurocentrism, which reveals their inextricable belief in their own monopoly on science, knowledge, leadership, expertise, finances, and / or power. Often displayed as egotism (a bourgeois European doctrine), these practices can be seen as endemic, essential, and acceptable "character flaws"—but they are inherently political. Most egomaniacs, of whatever "color," are expressing bourgeois individualism. Eurocentric egotists take up too much space displaying these characteristics in the context of collaborative possibilities with oppressed nationalities, weakening multinational, liberatory organization and Maroon community building.

The twenty-first century needs Maroons, including Maroon whites. Maroon whites want to leave the toxicity of American society—not believing it can be reformed or changed, even as a socialist society.

"Antiracist whites" may be satisfied with "activist" work, coalitions, united fronts, and mass work; Maroon whites will push these structures—with their Maroon comrades—toward more disciplined, highly accountable, soulful visionary formations designed to drive people beyond empire to more collective, humane, sustainable modes of living.

Maroon whites will join with oppressed nationalities— including national liberation movements of Native American nations, Puerto Ricans, Chican@ / Mexican@s, Black / New Afrikans, and others—in the desire to make a new identity, a new culture, a new relationship to Mother Earth that rejects the bourgeois European mentality of domination and control, a desire to create an entirely new humanity.

Maroon whites, if given the chance for reforms or improvements in American society that will split them from revolutionary Maroons as a whole, will reject these, remain part of the Maroon community as a whole, and never accept any invitations, bribes, inducements, and temptations to leave or betray their fellow Maroons.

Maroon whites will sacrifice their lives to defend their Maroon societies. Maroon whites won't assimilate into American anything. Maroon whites believe that the toxicity of white supremacy must never be allowed into the Maroon societies.

Maroon whites gladly accept an oppressed nationality majority. They shun white majorities everywhere. A Maroon society will never be a white majority, as Maroons are outlaws against the American mainstream.

Maroon whites believe oppressed nationality Maroons are their brothers and sisters, aunts and uncles, mothers and fathers, and would never betray them or give up this community for anything.

Maroon whites gladly work side by side with oppressed nationalities, will take the worst abuse from racist whites, and immerse themselves in the deepest Afro-Asian-Indigenous cultures.

Maroon whites do not accept or use terms like "people of color" or "minorities" or any nomenclature or appellation that the American mainstream preferences and promotes in pronouncements about their brother and sister Maroons.

Maroon whites don't accept anything white: white people, white culture, white history, white narratives, etc. Maroon whites learn about the world as it is, for which Europe and North America are indeed the true minorities. Maroon whites don't dress white, don't eat white, don't do anything white. They have ended whiteness in everything in their existence.

We require a world of Maroons—radical rejecters (not just resisters) ready to take on Empire, white supremacy, patriarchy, capitalism, and all oppressions, including the war being fought against the earth itself.

Maroons must work passionately together to build matriarchy, ecosocialism, and an end to "civilization" as we know it.

***

Commentary and clarifications: this article elicited much debate and discussion, online and otherwise. One respondent suggested that the construct of "Maroon whites" was not a liberation theology but a "reversal of oppression," because replacing patriarchy with matriarchy was just replacing one form of oppression with another (in the translation of "archy" as "rule by and power over"). Another critique suggested that we were pushing whites to reject everything about our identity in a reversal of what whites had "once upon a time" asked Blacks to do. The following clarifications were published online in the interest of furthering the discussion:

Ben Barson of Ecosocialist Horizons *wrote:*
"Archy" also means "consent to." Regardless, its etymology does not matter—your algebraic reversal of the roles of oppression shows how thoroughly you are entrapped in relations of domination. Human society, being for much of its existence matriarchal and matricentric, did not experience class society, gendered power differentials, bourgeois conceptions of family and ownership of spouses as property, etc. It was a communalistic commons in which humanity was integrated with nature and women were at the center of political and economic decisions.

As per your defense of "white" culture (as if there ever was such a thing), I'd like to refer you to James Baldwin. Those who became white, Baldwin wrote, did so at great expense:

> The crisis of leadership in the white community is remarkable—and terrifying—because there is, in fact, no white community.
>
> There is, for example—at least, in principle—an Irish community: here, there, anywhere, or more

precisely, Belfast, Dublin, Boston. There is an Italian community: Rome, Naples, the Bank of the Holy Ghost, and Mulberry Street. And there is a Jewish community, stretching from Jerusalem to California to New York. . . . There are Swiss consortiums. There are Poles: In Warsaw (where they would like us to be friends) and in Chicago (where because they are white we are enemies). There are, for that matter, Indian restaurants, and Turkish baths. There is the underworld—the poor (to say nothing of those who intend to become rich) are always with us but this does not describe a community. It bears terrifying witness to what happened to everyone who got here, and paid the price of the ticket. The price was to become "white." No one was white before he / she came to America. It took generations, and a vast amount of coercion, before this became a white country.

America became white—the people who, as they claim, "settled" the country became white—because of the necessity of denying the Black presence, and justifying the Black subjugation. No community can be based on such a principle—or, in other words, no community can be established on so genocidal a lie. White men—from Norway, for example, where they are *Norwegians*—became white: by slaughtering the cattle, poisoning the wells, torching the houses, massacring Native Americans, raping Black women.

—James Baldwin, "On Being White . . . and Other Lies"

Whiteness, to Baldwin, is not just a European identity destroyer. Whiteness is built on a specific foundation that makes it unacceptable to any civilized community. Accepting "white" as your organizing space, your identity, etc. is like saying you accept being an imperialist. Do you try to "anti-imperialize" the Empire? Or do you dismantle it? White identity is built on Empire; therefore, the destruction of whiteness and the destruction of Empire are the product and process of each other.

Mark Lance of the Institute for Anarchist Studies added:
I certainly agree with Baldwin (and Ben Barson) that there is no such thing as "white culture" aside from a late vague construction that is tied to imperialism and racism. But I don't see how that puts Ben in agreement with the initial article. That article assumes it and talks about it. How does one interpret the claim that one should reject white people, white culture, white history, and white narratives if none of these things exist?

Put another way—and this is as much a response to Matt and Fred (if I may): if there is no such thing as white culture, then there is also no such thing as Maroon culture. Indeed, the idea that Palestinians, Sikhs, Ethiopians, descendants of Mississippi slaves, Hmong, Australian Aboriginals, Tibetans, each of the First Nations of the Americas, etc. are all a culture is far less reasonable than that "whites" are. Of course, that is not to say that it might not be strategically useful to form particular groupings of people in resisting various aspects of oppression, but not only is there no such cultural group, it is clearly misguided to suppose that racism operates according to the same dynamics or that it is driven by the same forces in all cases. (The Ainu of Japan are pretty seriously marginalized and oppressed, and along familiar racist lines, but I trust we can't talk about "whiteness" there as if it is the same power structure as Western imperialism.) Further, any political program that is going to have the legitimacy to make specific demands about how others work in solidarity vis-à-vis all racially oppressed people will have to come from a pretty broad and representative group encompassing all these diverse peoples.

Sam Diener of the War Resisters League and American Friends Service Committee responded:
This is fascinating!

What I love about the Maroon metaphor is that it emphasizes the long history of escape from and resistance to enslavement and domination of all kinds and the importance of building communities of liberation and resistance with diverse allies. Your essay reminds me of the argument that Sara Evans makes in her book *Free Spaces* about the crucial role that liberated and liberating spaces can have for fostering movements for fundamental social change.

I also appreciate the importance of critiquing white antiracist practice: the question of what is effective work against racism, in this case when undertaken by white people, is a thorny one. As someone with white privilege struggling to be an effective antiracist ally and advocate of justice, I wrestle with these questions, and I don't think there are easy answers.

I'm bothered by a tone in this piece that seems to present an unnecessary binary choice: white antiracists bad, Maroon whites good. I know the piece doesn't necessarily say that all white antiracist practices are harmful (hence the repeated use of the phrase "white antiracists may . . ."), but I think too often what follows the "may" is a straw person argument that doesn't critique white antiracist practice itself but is an important critique of the positions of putatively liberal whites who profess, not even antiracism, but the ideology of "color-blind" nonracism.

Rather than characterizing people as good or bad, I want to learn from, honor, and build on a long line of flawed but important antiracist actions by people of all races, including a few white people, in North America and Europe. The earliest examples of white people working to end racism in the Americas I know of were in Cuba in the early 1500s: they were Jesuits who refused to give communion to any fellow Spaniard who practiced slavery. They in turn motivated the slave owner Bartolomé de las Casas to free the people he had enslaved and become a lifelong campaigner against racism against the Indigenous people of the Americas and advocate of human rights. His legacy, too, is quite mixed.

I wonder if one might regard some of the actions of Cabeza de Vaca and Thomas Morton as early exemplars of Maroon antiracism? Cabeza de Vaca was a Spanish would-be conquistador, who, after being shipwrecked multiple times in 1528, was himself enslaved for a time, according to his account, and then (after escaping) walked across the southwest part of what is now the U.S. and Northern Mexico. When, six years later, after living with a number of ethnic communities, he encountered Spaniards again, they were Spanish slave raiders whose crimes he strenuously objected to.

In the 1620s, in what is today Quincy, Massachusetts, Morton served as "host" of the Merrymount community, which worked closely with the Algonquin tribes of the area and spoke out against the racist, genocidal, and theocratic depredations of the Pilgrims and Puritans. Again, his legacy is mixed: among other things he still believed in spreading Christianity to Native peoples, but his attempts to build a multiracial community of resistance fascinate me.

Fred Ho reasserted:

1. The colonization of North America into the consolidation as the USA Empire has meant the de-ethnicization of *all* for the "price of the ticket" (James Baldwin) of entry into the American matrix. Therefore, Europeans *become* white in the context of becoming Americans. The continuation of African slavery today is the de-Africanization of Black people in becoming Americans, hence they wear straightened, pressed / processed hair, bourgeois business suits, eat the worst food from slavery days (and call it "soul food"), etc.

2. The Empire is now consolidated, spanning across the globe, including territories in the Caribbean and Pacific Ocean (including the U.S.'s fiftieth state). Maroon societies were *stamped out.* Our call, or manifesto, is to regenerate them. We need new revolutionary Maroon identities, spaces, kreolization, etc., to resist the Empire's imposed identity and allegiance.

3. Matrifocal, matricentric, matrilineal, all combined, is both the old ancient matriarchy and the new, coming-into-being revolutionary matriarchy. Ancient matriarchies continue, though diluted due to capitalist globalization, with the Iroquois, the Minangkabau, the Wayuu—in every part of the globe—but they are Indigenous, local subsistence-local production–based societies, not global empires or nation-states.

4. Whiteness is pure fabrication. What is its music? What is its cuisine? What is its clothing? What is its history? All expropriations, the plunder of conquest and subjugation, and the lies of White mythologies. When people naively cite pizza or spaghetti, I point out that these are originally Chinese, and not Italian!

5. The practice of Marooning is like the practice of commoning: it must be brought about through opposition and continued colonization / captivity by the American matrix. The Black, Chicano, and Native liberation struggles all seek to dismember and delink from the U.S. Empire. Are "whites" helping? Are *you* helping? Or are *you* promoting assimilation and integrationism?

Matt Meyer concluded:

This piece is an intentional polemic, one of the few I have ever allowed my name to be included on in almost forty years of involvement in social change movements. I generally agree that one must avoid "unnecessary binary choices" and struggle against many false dichotomies, including the various Martin-Malcolm divides. Here, however, we wished to provide a jumping-off point to provoke more widespread discussion, and in that sense it has already succeeded as evidenced by the above comments. Hopefully, this discussion will be extended further in the years to come.

A few things, in hindsight, clearly need to be added:

1. Building broad and representative groupings—organizations in some cases, as well as united fronts and coalitions—remains an urgent task, one that Scientific Soul Sessions (SSS) failed to achieve. But our attempts did achieve more than just some interesting ideas or even some long-standing comradely relationships that exist across organizational lines to this day. When the National Campaign to Free Russell Maroon Shoatz swung into full gear, for example, it was with SSS cadre at the center; Fred Ho was chief benefactor and strategist, Theresa Shoatz was national spokesperson, and I served as national organizer in an eighteen-month project that

eventually forced Pennsylvania to let Maroon out of solitary confinement after twenty-two torturous consecutive years. Our success was not, as a recent article in *The Nation* would have it, due primarily to legal maneuvers or to the die-hard commitment of Maroon's faithful family (though those two elements, always recognized as important aspects of the campaign, certainly played a role). It was due to a strategic sizing up of some fundamental facts regarding how to make Maroon's continued solitary confinement more "expensive" to the Pennsylvania Department of Corrections than it was worth. Maroon's own continued brilliance as a thinker and world analyst was vital here; he remains the chief inspiration for this article and for many movement youth on both sides of the wall. Publishing and widely distributing his writings were core parts of our campaign, as was a major national book tour that doubled as an organizing tour—getting local groups of many varieties to send emails, make phone calls, fax support letters, and hold demonstrations whenever we needed to let the Pennsylvania authorities know we were raising the stakes for Maroon. Pushing hard on international solidarity, including the support of three Nobel Peace Prize recipients, played a role, as did growing support among artists, especially in but not limited to the New Black Arts Movement. Folks like Kanya D'Almeida, Quincy Saul, and countless other cadre and part-time supporters built local, regional, national, and global ties that ultimately made the continued torture of Maroon more of an embarrassing headache than the Pennsylvania Department of Corrections wished to bear. The idea that one could become a "Maroon white" played a motivational role in this, especially for those looking for concrete ways out of the morass of stultifying white supremacy.

2. The idea of "special antiracist white people" is still a controversial one, as extraordinary leaders of the Black Liberation Movement assert their importance in certain key instances. I was privileged to sit on a panel with former Black Panther political prisoner Sekou Odinga at a spring 2016 Black Lives Matter strategy session, where Odinga argued that there were a few—both of us agreeing that our dear comrade David Gilbert, a political prisoner since 1980 for his solidarity with the Black struggles of the 1960s and beyond, was a key case in point. David would be the first, loudest, and longest to assert that there was a problem in viewing some whites as especially antiracist, but ironically the fact that David considers himself little different than the many Black, Puerto Rican, Mexican, Indigenous, and others who have given their lives to the struggle is one of the things that makes him, as the last remaining white anti-imperialist political prisoner of that historic period, quite special and different indeed. My fundamental point is this: no person raised white under white supremacy, like no one raised male under patriarchy, can—whatever the acts, thoughts, or decades in the struggle—completely extinguish from every fiber of our psyche all forms of supremacist attitudes. Thus, when the inevitable mistake, mess up, or problem comes, let us and those we work in solidarity with understand the context and respond accordingly. All people make mistakes of one kind or another, and there is clearly specialness in people of all ethnicities, cultures, etc. In regard to principled unity across all lines—ideological, religious, geographic, and gender-based—Sekou perhaps put it

best when he was reflecting on the lessons of the FBI's illegal Counterintelligence Program (COINTELPRO), which helped to destroy the Panthers. COINTELPRO helped encourage us to look so sharply at the reasons for us to divide, and Odinga suggests that now it is our duty to look more urgently at our points of agreement, our reasons to unite.

3. Finally, I am struck by a term being suggested by indigenous African feminist Bernadette Muthien, who is researching and writing about "*rematriation*." In a rematriated construct, Muthien writes, "identities may be seen as heterogeneous, fluid, and dynamic—but must first be situated in their social-historical contexts to be understood and respected. The introduction of a rematriated type of Love (which suggests the interconnectedness of all things) will enable us to inquire into femininities, sexualities, and ancient spiritualities." This context also allows for radically transformed power dynamics on both the personal and political levels.

Strategic Alliance Building
A Change Is Gonna Come

Anniversaries seem like "teachable moment" times—when folks can more easily reflect on what things we did well or poorly.

Toward the end of 2017, commemorations were taking place of the fiftieth anniversary of the popularization of the slogan "Black Power"—often attributed to Stokely Carmichael of SNCC. Stokely's closest running mate—from the SNCC years through his time in the Black Panthers, from his name change to Kwame Ture to the development of the All-African People's Revolutionary Party (AAPRP)—was the organizer's organizer: Bob Brown. Brown and I met in 1981, when I was a nineteen-year-old draft registration resister looking to learn from anyone willing to teach. Bob and his AAPRP comrade Mawina Sowa Kouyate did so much more than that. The two joined the national and New York staff of the peace coalition known as Mobilization for Survival, and—along with many others—we helped build for the million-person-strong UN and Central Park–based disarmament demonstration in 1982 that turned out to be the largest peace march in U.S. history. Under the leadership of Leslie Cagan, we pushed for every sector of U.S. life, every possible constituency, to come out to ensure that the "fate of the earth" would not be nuclear winter and that U.S. economic policy would be transformed to "meet human needs." Under Bob and Mawina's tutelage and later meeting and traveling to North Africa with Kwame himself, I learned of an Africa that was "on the move" and envisioned a Pan-African unity that could help steer the world off its apparent collision course.

Reflecting on Black Power's fiftieth and our own thirty-fifth anniversary of the great New York City peace march, Bob noted that Kwame often spoke of the campaigns and slogans that he was most proud of—that were most central in actually building for lasting social change. It turns out that Kwame's popularization of the antiwar, antidraft cry, "Hell No, We Won't Go!" meant more to him in some ways than even "Black Power." It was the former, Kwame reflected, that helped bring together white antidraft activists and Black and Latino antiwar youth in a series of campaigns that helped halt the war and end the draft itself.

In commemorating fifty years, we asked Leslie and several student and youth representatives to join us for reflections on the future.

For me, it was a chance to reiterate and sharpen some basic themes of our work.

***

It was, indeed, 1967 when Sergeant Pepper taught the Beatles to play, and they taught the rest of us how to fully redefine a generation and mass culture as a whole. Aretha spelled out her demand for R-E-S-P-E-C-T, and Buffalo Springfield, for what it's worth, sang that "something's happening here, but what it is ain't exactly clear."

Some people, however—including Rev. Dr. Martin Luther King, Jr.—suggested that things were in fact getting very much clearer. Dr. King, with a little help from his friends, proclaimed his independence from the civil rights conservatives when he publicly questioned: "What do the Vietnamese people think as we test out our latest weapons on them just as the Germans tested out new medicines and new tortures in the concentration camps of Europe?"

In calling for a true revolution, Dr. King's true friends included Dr. Vincent Harding, who helped write his historic "Beyond Vietnam" speech, from which that quote comes, and Stokely Carmichael, who was sitting among the first rows of Riverside Church, cheering King on as he delivered it. Perhaps more than any other leader of his time or since, Stokely embodies a nexus between Martin and Minister Malcolm X, between the strategic nonviolence of voter registration and the tactical arms carried by the Black Panthers for self-defense and defense of a people. Stokely was both chairman of the Student Nonviolent Coordinating Committee and, just a few years later, honorary prime minister of the Black Panther Party.

Fast forward fifteen years. When Bob, Leslie, and I first met, I was serving as the national representative of the U.S. Student Association and the Progressive Student Network to the June 12, 1982 mobilization. The huge numbers that day were the result of not one but three distinct coalitions organizing for the event, which is why even now some revisionist histories will falsely tell you that the demonstration was only for a nuclear freeze—which is like writing, as one prominent pacifist recently did for a major nonviolence-oriented website, that Dr. King was essentially a conservative thinker, the pacifist writer's thesis based solely on King's writings and actions up until 1963.

It has long been my assertion that we re-assassinate King annually each January when we freeze-frame him as if the years 1963–1968 never took place. We do similar injustices to all of our movement histories when we tell convenient lies or engage in the omissions that distort how real and ordinary people engage in very real organizing to make real and extraordinary social change.

Reflecting on our movements and our own pasts in order to reaffirm our vital alliances today and imagine more effective work in the future, there are two revisionist history myths that are in dire need of myth busting. The *first myth* intended to keep us from effective organizing is that Black people—maybe especially Stokely Carmichael, followed by many others—ordered white folks out of the civil rights and social justice movements, forced them out of SNCC, and generally brought about a dissolution of the "beloved community" that was coming together at that time. The legacy is clear, and it is based on a premise as false as it is destructive. The *fact* is that the Atlanta Project of SNCC, recognizing that the main group representing Black students had a number of white activists within it, set about a controversial challenge: white students interested in justice should focus their work in their own communities, thus also enabling students of African descent to take the unencumbered lead in theirs. There would be no bars to alliances, friendships, or strategic coalitions; there would just be a logical division of work and leadership. But logic and strategic action has not been a strong suit of the U.S. left, especially when it involves people of European descent giving up leadership and power.

To be sure, when I first met both Bob and Leslie I was eager to learn everything I could about the people's movements and the alliances between Kwame's people and the next generation who led the Vietnam antiwar movement. The AAPRP had joined the coalition known as Mobilization for Survival, led by Leslie, and AAPRP militants Bob Brown and Mawina Sowa Kouyate of the All-African Women's Revolutionary Union took positions on Mobe's national and New York staff. As mentioned above, I was truly embraced and mentored by Mawina and Bob, and later the same would be true of Pan-African pacifist Bill Sutherland, who had left the U.S. altogether in 1953, living his days as an unflinching supporter of the African liberation movements and an unofficial people's ambassador between the continent and the diaspora.

In part, those connections were personal and individual, but they were also very political in nature; I can't imagine that the AAPRP did all the work with us they did primarily because they liked Leslie or me so much. There was always at the center of things a deep commitment to internationalism. It was and is an internationalism that understands that the U.S. is more of an empire and prison house of internal and external colonies than it is a simple nation-state with so-called racial minorities like Puerto Ricans (who, I can say from my time there celebrating the release of patriot Oscar López Rivera, very much think that Puerto Rico is their own country) or Mexicans (who have had borders and fences and walls built around them long before the current president suggested new construction). It is an internationalism centered on Pan-Africanism, which includes Africans in the U.S., who are part of a mighty diaspora. And it is an internationalism that has never neglected the struggles of Indigenous peoples, the Palestinians, and others and that still provides, in my estimate, some of the most vital lessons for our collective future.

So, no, Kwame Ture and the inheritors of his legacy were and are not responsible for the splits between "Black" and "white" but are, rather, exemplars of radical alliance building.

The *second destructive myth* we need to focus on involves that nexus between Martin and Malcolm and what some of us are now calling the false dichotomy between revolutionary violence and nonviolence. Despite differences between them, they both seemed to have a much less difficult time dealing with those who didn't agree with them tactically, strategically, or philosophically. Their pre–Vietnam War era vision of anti-imperialism and revolutionary aspiration understood that alliances had to be built well beyond pacifists, peaceniks, and the middle class. Labor union militants and students had to be key elements of any effective mass movement. And coalition building by definition meant working closely with people whom one didn't agree with on some fundamental issues.

Bill Sutherland perhaps put it most clearly: it was not his job, even as a person of African descent who had dedicated his life to the liberation movements, to tell the peoples of Namibia or Zambia or Algeria or anywhere how best to wage their struggle. That arrogance was a part of the Eurocentric paternalism he had sought to leave behind. In fact, Bill felt that it was his and our main job to get the boot of U.S. imperial, capitalist aggression off the backs of all the peoples of Africa and the Global South. As part of the War Resisters' International and the Quaker-based American Friends Service Committee, Bill fought long and hard to ensure that all liberation movements received dedicated solidarity. He would, to be sure, support grassroots nonviolent efforts when they emerged. But, as the literal host to both Martin Luther King, Jr., in Ghana, and Malcolm X, in Tanzania, he refused to choose, on a personal as well as a political level, between two essential, strategic positions that might both be necessary in overcoming the forces of reaction.

Today, we may surely need to explore greater, more creative, and more militant forms of revolutionary nonviolence, but it is at best a dead end to preach that nonviolence (or armed struggle for that matter) is the *only* means to the revolution we clearly need.

Today, technology allows us to communicate more quickly and efficiently with larger groups of people across longer distances and across cultural and economic divides. More than language or money, we need the political will and acumen to build the kind of diverse and decisive coalitions that could turn the tide away from the reactionary regimes of late neoliberalism. Some of that can emerge from the long-lasting alliances forged after decades of trusted collaborative work. Some of that acumen can develop from scientific socialist analysis based on decades of real-world organization-to-organization party building. And some of the passion, energy, and creativity needed can be built from the visions, poetry, and power of new voices and new generations.

Forward ever! A change is surely gonna come.

REDEFINING REVOLUTION AND NONVIOLENCE
REIMAGINING SOLIDARITY ACROSS RACE, CLASS, GENDER, AND GENERATIONS

IF WE ARE TO TAKE "RACE," CLASS, AND PATRIARCHY WITHin the USA and the U.S. empire seriously in the context of a world with many centers and multiple imperialistic and oppressive forces of attack against people's movements (and just plain people), we will have to carefully redefine our terms.

It is not simply that the USA has, for some time, not been a place where "Black and white" adequately describe racial, ethnic, or experiential cultural differences between people. And it is not merely that contemporary critiques of gender binary systems make a "male-female" dichotomy less central to some liberation struggles than it used to be. Redefining our terms and realities may have more to do with class—a concept that in the USA (including the U.S. left) has never been taken particularly seriously. How else can we explain the consistency with which poor white folks act / organize / vote / think against their own basic, long-term interests?

I believe we must do more than simply dramatically and creatively reintroduce nuanced concepts of class into the work of the left. I believe that other concepts—most specifically, *solidarity, nonviolence,* and *revolution*—need a redefined and rehabilitated overhaul if progressives in the

USA are to have any chance of gaining ground (as we have failed to do for fifty years).

So let us be as specific—as literal and clear and intentional—as possible in the words we use and how we define them.

When we say "revolution," what most often comes to mind is fighting, violence, guns, and death. When we say "nonviolence," people often think of passivity (as in passivism not pacifism), of witness, of purity and absolutism, of sitting in rather than standing up, and of being completely nonconfrontational.

The great mistake regarding *all* of these descriptors of nonviolence is that they go against the basic precepts of what most well-known nonviolent leaders of the past half century believed in: Gandhi was all about confronting the British; King believed in a moral arc but not in absolutist adherence to anything. And it wasn't just Gandhi who believed that love force needed to be central to our struggle. Cuba's Che Guevara, leader of military units not just in Latin America but throughout Africa, famously noted that every true revolutionary must act out of great love for the people.

Noting these realities, some of us have suggested an ideological marriage of Gandhi and Che, the need for new ideological development of a Revolutionary Nonviolence.

U.S. feminist and civil rights activist Barbara Deming, who advocated anything but passivity and witness, pressed for "Revolution and Equilibrium" in a classic essay that engaged with the writings of African armed struggle advocate Frantz Fanon. Fanon, a psychiatrist originally from Martinique, suggested that a cathartic violence on the part of the oppressed might be necessary to throw off the yoke of psychological oppression embedded in the "wretched of the earth." Deming suggested there was something unbalanced with a sharp disconnect between the ends and the means of one's struggle—and that the experiments in radical nonviolence, which had barely begun, needed to continue to work toward that balance. Deming was clear: "Nonviolence has for too long been connected in people's minds with the notion of passivity. . . . . The challenge to those who believe in nonviolent struggle is to learn to be aggressive enough." In addition, as—first and foremost—an activist and advocate on the side of the oppressed, Deming knew that "[i]t is not possible to act at all and to remain pure—and that is not what I want when I commit myself to the nonviolent discipline. I stand with all" who are ready to act against oppression and injustice.

The power of nonviolence may appear to be about doing away with violence, but in fact any radical movement that challenges the status quo and state power is going to face repression, violence, death, and possibly war. What an adherence to nonviolence suggests, however, is that those who practice and experiment with it may well be on the receiving end of violence but will be very hesitant indeed to use it strategically and tactically to wage struggle. Practitioners of a revolutionary nonviolence will understand clearly that while we must expect and prepare for (and even allow for defense against) vicious and violent attacks, our own use of violent tactics usually involves a long-term terrible price.

It is difficult for militarism not to creep in to our ideologies and practice. It is difficult for us to do as the great African liberation commander Amílcar Cabral taught: "Tell no lies, claim no easy victories." The famous speech that concluded with those lines was actually a strong push for the soldiers under Cabral's command to be, in his words, "militants but never militarists." Cabral's vehement calls to oppose all militarism and violence may seem strange to those with a less nuanced view of revolution, but they fall perfectly in line with an understanding that, while in some situations it may seem that armed force is needed within a revolutionary context, glorification of weaponry and the military has never been an effective revolutionary strategy.

When we seek to redefine and clarify our definitions of solidarity and alliance, we must begin by being clear that solidarity cannot succeed if it is merely aid from one privileged group to an "underprivileged" group, not tender loving care from those in power to the beggars and destitute. Solidarity must stem from a radical critique of the historic dynamics of race, class, and patriarchy and must be based on respect for the self-determination of all people.

We must ponder how best to reimagine solidarity as the great African anticolonial freedom fighter Samora Machel of Mozambique did, as two fists striking a single blow against a common, oppressive enemy.

OSCAR LÓPEZ RIVERA
AMERICA'S MANDELA AND HIS
MOVEMENT FACE THE FUTURE

ANA LÓPEZ AND MATT MEYER

No greater, more nuanced, complicated, or successful solidarity effort preoccupied the last two decades of my life than the movement to free Puerto Rican political prisoner Oscar López Rivera, and—through those efforts—to help free Puerto Rico, one of the last direct colonies on the face of the earth and the fundamental responsibility of all the people of the USA. This essay, written with the coordinator of the New York City branch of the campaign, shares our perspectives on the strategies and tactics of twenty-first-century solidarity: an insider's view of the nuances behind the winning campaign. Since Oscar's release in May of 2017, the devastating effects of economic destabilization, hurricane, climate crisis, and colonialism have sharpened the solidarity dynamics facing the Puerto Rican movement. With a commander in chief reinforcing some of the most racist hyperbole about Puerto Rican laziness (reminiscent of pushes for the oppressed to "pick themselves up by their bootstraps"), many U.S. citizens recognized for the first time that Puerto Ricans were citizens, too, albeit ones who can be drafted to fight in U.S. wars but are not eligible to vote for U.S. presidents or congressional representatives.

Part 1: The Man

Puerto Rican community and pro-independence leader Oscar López Rivera has been widely recognized as the "Nelson Mandela of the Americas." Several Latin American heads of state originally bestowed that title on him at the 2015 Organization of American States summit—though López Rivera has for decades also enjoyed the staunch support of close Mandela associate Archbishop Desmond Tutu, the South African Nobel Peace laureate who headed that country's Truth and Reconciliation Commission. López Rivera, like Mandela, served most of his adult life behind bars, charged with the thought crime of "seditious conspiracy" for fighting for the freedom of his people. At age seventy-four, and after more than thirty-five years behind bars, López Rivera was the political prisoner with the distinction of being the longest held in the history of Puerto Rican-U.S. colonial relations.

Born in San Sebastian, Puerto Rico, in 1943, López Rivera moved to the U.S. at age fourteen with his family, settling in the Puerto Rican community of Humboldt Park, Chicago. As a young adult he was drafted into the U.S. military and sent to fight in the front lines of Vietnam, where he was awarded the Bronze Star for heroic service. Returning to Chicago in 1967, he was quickly politicized by the movements for social change he encountered. López Rivera became involved with many community empowerment groups, eventually helping to found the award-winning alternative Dr. Pedro Albizu Campos High School. Along with his brother, José, López Rivera also helped found Chicago's Puerto Rican Cultural Center. Aware of the developing revolutionary processes in Puerto Rico and in countries throughout the Global South, he eventually decided to join the clandestine movement, becoming a part of the Fuerzas Armadas de Liberación Nacional Puertorriqueña (FALN).

Arrested in 1981, López Rivera declared himself to be an anticolonial combatant entitled to the protection of international law (as did his colleagues arrested in 1980 and 1983), challenging the jurisdiction of the U.S. courts to criminalize efforts against colonialism, since colonialism is itself a crime against humanity. Nevertheless, the court still handed out politically punitive sentences—almost seven times longer than the average sentence for violent offenses during that time, though none of those put on trial were convicted of harming or killing anyone. Once imprisoned, López Rivera faced years of torture, what he has termed "spiriticide," including sensory deprivation, more than twelve years of solitary confinement, and subjugation to the supermaximum security practices of the prisons within a prison at Marion (Illinois) and ADX Florence (Colorado).

Perhaps the most striking similarity between Oscar López Rivera and South African former president Mandela is the humanity and strength of spirit developed and maintained during their long decades of incarceration. In addition to his correspondence and writing activities, his avid reading, and a turn toward vegetarianism, López Rivera became a skillful artist, painting portraits and tributes to his native homeland. His work has been exhibited throughout the world, sponsored in part by the international human rights campaign. López Rivera authored numerous articles that have inspired many generations; in the last years before his release, he helped produce two books of his writings: *Between Torture and Resistance* (PM Press, 2013) and *Cartas a Karina* (CAK Project, 2016), which was short-listed for the Eric Hoffer Book Award for independent publishing.

Over the decades, Puerto Rico–based marches focusing on Oscar and other political prisoners mobilized hundreds of thousands. Support for Oscar created a unity that included all political tendencies and elected officials of every political party throughout the island. The "Oscar in the Street" campaign placed life-size cutout photos of López Rivera on walls and balconies throughout the island. And a women-centered campaign of flash demonstrations sprung up in major cities throughout Puerto Rico and the diaspora. Nobel Peace Prize winners from every continent, ultimately numbering over a dozen, sent letters, videos, and personal messages. They participated in prayer vigils calling for López Rivera's unconditional release—as did prominent religious, labor, and political leaders throughout the U.S., and such artists as Lin-Manuel Miranda, Calle 13's Rene Pérez, and Ricky Martin (to mention a few). In a session of the United Nations Committee on Decolonization just months before Obama granted the commutation, an unprecedented and historic forty-plus representatives of countries and peoples' movements joined the call, with the UN Committee itself officially stating that its members would visit Oscar in prison.

A transcendent figure in contemporary Puerto Rican life, Oscar López Rivera surprised few with his personal plan after prison to develop the Fundación Oscar López Rivera-Libertá, which will deepen the unity and work for decolonization that has been the cornerstone of his entire existence.

Part 2: The Movement

At a planning meeting for Oscar's first freedom visit to New York City following his release, the very concrete connections between the personal and the political hit home to both of the authors of this article. Over the course of the campaign to free Oscar and all of the beloved political prisoners of his generation, one young participant in that meeting had literally grown up in our midst. The representative of the Betances Community Center spoke of the teachers who had inspired her from high school to college and beyond, and Meyer and López—both of us in the room—listened with pride to our former student as she referenced our work with her. Though the passing from one classroom to the next was far from intentional (we work at opposite ends of our vast city in completely distinct and unconnected institutions), the sociocultural ties that bind over a lifetime of struggle run deep. And Oscar—the man and the movement—has occupied almost the entirety of our adult lives, along with the lives of our students, our spouses and children, and our friends, as organizers and humanitarians.

It is the magnetism of the movement that draws us in, a heartfelt alternative to the corruption of mainstream imperial society that surrounds us. Leading our lives as part of the freedom movement means traveling the road to truth and justice—a road that we believe all humans are, in their hearts, searching for. It is the struggle for truth and justice that makes us feel good and happy as a people. When the opposite of those things is what surrounds us instead, we get diseased in personal and political ways, with fiscal and physical infirmities, on emotional and social levels. By making history through the Oscar campaign and other campaigns that preceded it—freeing Puerto Rican patriots who, when first incarcerated, seemed isolated and never likely to see the light of day again—we have collectively changed and corrected the course of our history. If we learn the lessons of these social-change struggles, we can move forward and not repeat the horrors of the past.

Reflecting upon our decades of struggle, building a free-dom movement that was centered around individuals behind bars but was also always extended to the aspirations of libera-tion of an entire people, three key aspects of the work deserve to be highlighted at this crucial, celebratory time.

First: so many movements to free political prisoners in the U.S. suffer from a lack of understanding on the most practical of levels of the power and necessity for tight, vision-ary, unified, and principled organization. If a tiny group of extremely dedicated people just worked a little harder, it is sometimes falsely suggested, our elders would be free.

Time and time again, at public forums and in private conversations, the work of our tireless and stalwart lawyers is praised, and the sacrifices of the families of those whom the empire would leave rot in their dungeons is righteously spotlighted. Both of these commendations are correct. But lawyers and family members, though central to the spirit and practical aspects of all freedom campaigns, almost never win victories on their own. The very best lawyers working nonstop around the clock, paired with the hardest working family members dedicated to their loved ones, still cannot free those behind bars without well-coordinated strategic campaigns led by consistent organizers and organizations.

Sadly, and much to our long-term weakening, the art and skill of organizing is disappearing. Organizers are devalued, as if anyone can do it naturally, as if no training or experience is needed or helpful, as if our good intentions, intense feel-ings, or prayer alone will bring about radical transformation. Building long-term, successful campaigns, however, takes strategic planning and the ability to be open and flexible over time. It takes a variety of tactics that, while not always appar-ently working in tandem, at least do not directly contradict one another. It takes simple and patient, not always sexy or spotlighted, person-to-person contact. This means meeting people where they're at, not making them use forms unfamiliar to them. For some, this means social media in short, simple tweets; for others, it means door-to-door neighborhood and street corner conversations about why A led to B or why person X was involved in activity Z.

Dr. Luis Nieves Falcón of the Campaign for Human Rights in San Juan and Professor José E. López of the Juan Antonio Corretjer Puerto Rican Cultural Center in Chicago were two of the most significant leaders of the campaign to free Oscar and the campaigns to free all Puerto Rican political prisoners. There can be little question that Nieves Falcón was vital to the work, in part because of his coordination of an expert legal team. He made a now legendary decision to leave a comfortable life as University of Puerto Rico sociologist and department chair of the Center for Caribbean and Latin American Studies to go back to school and become a lawyer for the sole purpose of defending the incarcerated prisoners. But there can be equally little question that Nieves Falcón's main contribution was not that of a lawyer. The significance of José López's intense dedication to his older brother Oscar cannot be overstated. But it would be foolishness itself to suggest that José's main contributions to his brother's freedom were centered around his efforts as a dedicated sibling.

Luis Nieves Falcón and José López were and are master strategists; their leadership as organizers, political thinkers, coalition builders, and inspiring educator-speakers far, far exceeds their work as lawyer and family member. Oscar was blessed not only with a strength of spirit and political clarity that kept him shrewd and smart throughout the torture and confusion but also with people who were family members, true friends, lawyers, organizers, and supporters all at the same time. Everyone involved became members of the family both literally and figuratively.

One lesson of the Oscar campaign that must exist beyond the myth—and beyond Oscar's personal freedom—is that any and every successful campaign needs to be built on solid organization, led by organizers who can ride the waves of sectarianism, government repression, a fickle and sometimes hostile media, and politicians who can be both useful and obstructionist. We were flexible enough to hold together an all-inclusive, multifaceted, long-term campaign in which no one had to give up their individual ideologies so long as they agreed—on at least a humanitarian level—to fight for Oscar's freedom "with one voice."

The second aspect worth noting is that in the campaign for Oscar's release the central organizers were "neither insiders nor outsiders" to the political process surrounding us.

Perhaps the most controversial part of the Oscar movement was its reliance in its final phases on dedicated elected officials who went far beyond what the average politician is ever likely to do. New York's City Council Speaker Melissa Mark-Viverito, San Juan's Mayor Carmen Yulín, and Chicago's Congressman Luis Gutiérrez were but a few of a growing number of government representatives who truly represented the wishes of their constituents and worked for Oscar's release from within city, state, and national offices. The authors of this article, as individuals and members of the New York Free Oscar Coordination Group, are not and have not been involved in electoral politics, are not and have not been supporters of the Democratic Party or any other electoral formation, and have in no way abandoned our commitment to the radical changes that we know will be required if there is to be true justice and peace in the world.

At the same time, we are not so arrogant or sectarian as to believe that everyone agrees or needs to agree with these perspectives or work modes in order to be part of a given campaign. In addition, we understand that the historic moment in which we work has, at times, benefited from the support of some elected officials in Puerto Rico and the U.S. The freedom campaign that resulted in the release of twelve Puerto Rican patriots in 1999 certainly did. This is not to say that those elected officials can or should be automatically seen as leading or being the spokespeople for such campaigns—a very tricky and sensitive reality given how ego-driven mainstream society and electoral politics have become. A balancing act is needed whereby elected officials must be accountable to people's movements, as all *should* be in any even remotely democratic society. The media, and far too frequently our movement colleagues, often substitute these officials for campaign strategists as our public face—a dangerous game given how demobilizing and disempowering electoral politics has been to people's movements throughout modern times.

We nevertheless must recognize the difference between careerists and sellouts, on the one hand, and those rare elected officials who for decades have remained part of and true to the movement, on the other (including Representative Gutiérrez, who came up as an organizer for Chicago's Puerto Rican Community Center, or Speaker Mark-Viverito, who came up through New York's ASPIRA). This includes recognizing that, as elected officials, they may be called upon to make compromises that our movements cannot agree with or find acceptable. In that case, we must critique them as needed, without losing sight of the contributions they may still make to a given campaign. We must view these elected allies through a different lens, understanding that their emergence within the mainstream systems only takes place because of openings and windows that the people themselves have created within a particular historical context.

We are reminded of a single moment, over seventeen years ago, before the release of the twelve. Some campaign contacts had enough "insider" connections to obtain a White House meeting for a small group of our leaders and lawyers with President Clinton's pardon attorney. At the same time, many in the campaign felt that we had exhausted every option—from petitions and letters to street actions and prayer vigils and more. Sixteen Puerto Rican political prisoners languished behind bars at the time, and a tightly planned group of sixteen of us, along with several hundred others, organized a confrontation at the gates in front of the White House. The civil disobedience in which our group was arrested linked Puerto Rican community leaders, including the coordinator of the National Boricua Human Rights Network, with Plowshares activists and war resisters more familiar with nonviolent direct action. It was coalition building in at least three directions—with arrests taking place in front of the White House literally at the same time as some of our comrades were having a meeting inside of it.

Too many among the broadest ranges of the Oscar campaign have taken the extreme positions of either following our elected officials as if they are our ultimate decision-making leaders or refusing to work with them in any way because they are part of the "establishment." For us, both extremes are too limiting. Electoral politics in this day and age can be no more or less than a tactic to be used effectively, presuming we do not expect too much or decry it too much.

Still others are, in our opinion, too enamored of direct action—thinking that only rhetorical displays of our militant positions will show our power (when in fact they sometimes do the opposite, showing how foolish and weak a tiny group of shouting demonstrators can be). We must be dialectical and mature enough to understand that no revolutionary transformation has ever taken place without a diversity of strategies and tactics.

The third and final key organizing note is that the success of the Oscar campaign was largely based on consistently coordinated connections, from the grassroots to the international and back again. Though the success of the campaign would not have been possible without a strong foundation within local communities throughout Puerto Rico, the dynamism that inspired a give-and-take between the grassroots and international solidarity made success much more likely.

Let us begin to center this point around our clear analysis that the freedom of Oscar López Rivera, like the release of other imprisoned *independentistas* and nationalists of previous years, is one borne of the sacrifice, dedication, struggle, and consistent commitment of the Puerto Rican people, from the grassroots on up, from the island to the diaspora. No amount of even the most dedicated international solidarity could have come close to winning these victories if not for the massive and largely unwavering efforts of Puerto Ricans themselves—not always making up a numerical majority of the Puerto Rican population but always remaining connected to neighborhood-based, people-centered needs and concerns. This echoes our first point about the building of strong organizations and the first part of this essay, which speaks of Oscar's politics: an individual less committed to or reflective of the needs and concerns of the people would not have received the outpouring of love and support that Oscar got and so justly deserves.

The 32 Women for Oscar grew strong in Puerto Rico at a time when the economic measures of a bankrupt island were having a devastating impact on all people, most intensely affecting the majority-female population and all the children they were responsible for. During Oscar's last years in prison, domestic violence had been on the rise, and a mass exodus from the island had caused disruptions of families—along with the economic and land base they represent. Modeled after Latin American women's movements of past decades, the female voices for Oscar helped make visible not only Oscar but also themselves. In January 2014, a delegation of the thirty-two women came to New York, asking if women here wanted to create their own, similar organization. The challenge was accepted, and "Women for Oscar" vigils became a ritual throughout the city, rotating locations in different communities and raising awareness about Oscar and the situation in Puerto Rico. As part and parcel of the grassroots organizing, these women learned from one another how to become an effective, unified voice despite their different ideological viewpoints.

When the economic crisis became more severe, the Women for Oscar became a voice for everyone. Oscar's release gave us a glimpse to of all the possibilities we can build toward. Women in New York, and later Chicago and elsewhere, linked Puerto Rico with the diaspora in ways that allow us to organize more effectively for decolonization, to broaden, and to grow.

The Oscar campaign as a whole self-consciously linked grassroots community work like this to an international solidarity effort that was schooled in taking leadership directly from the Puerto Rican movement. This solidarity, respectful of and directed by the Puerto Rican leaders, was a vital element that helped give the movement some needed backup. It fueled the grassroots, who became energized by a recognition that the whole world was, in fact, watching. "Taking leadership" in this sense did not mean some kind of blind obedience to one Puerto Rican organization or another; it meant a creative engagement regarding how the work could be most effectively built in a wide variety of cultures, languages, and environments. It involved thinking strategically, with flexibility and a long-term approach, about how broadening the campaign could be done in ways that would not dilute the message or priorities of the man or of the movement.

In its essence, this meant adhering to precepts of self-determination. Ultimately, it has meant the building of life-long relationships of love, respect, and revolution.

At times, the international campaign meant long nights writing meticulous emails, or very early mornings making long-distance phone calls to faraway places. At others times, it meant introducing Oscar's daughter Clarissa to Nobel Peace laureate Archbishop Desmond Tutu in St. George's Anglican Cathedral in Cape Town, South Africa. It meant going barefoot at an Indian ashram, handing out fliers with Oscar's perfect painting of Mohandas Gandhi, getting notable figures including Gandhi's granddaughter to be strong supporters of the campaign. It meant dressing up to meet the Venezuelan ambassador to the United Nations, who headed that body's Decolonization Committee, or dressing comfortably to join a delegation to Nicaragua where a gathering of Latin American popular movements was being held (watching as nationalist icon and former prisoner of war Don Rafael Cancel Miranda explained to the border guards that he was a special guest of the conference but had only his Puerto Rican "passport" as far as official documents were concerned; he would not hold or travel on the passport of the colonizers).

International solidarity almost always meant adhering to a two-way-street analysis, understanding all we had to gain from giving. The peoples of Mauritius, the Indian Ocean island nation at the center of efforts to decolonize and demilitarize the island of Diego Garcia, which the U.S. Navy uses as a nuclear base and bombing range, were among the first to get in touch with us upon hearing of Oscar's clemency. They held "welcome home Oscar" celebrations that made the links between decolonization for both islands. East Timorese President José Ramos-Horta, the Nobel Prize–winning UN official who has long supported Oscar's freedom, consistently writes and talks about the connections between the role of militants and political prisoners in Puerto Rico and his Pacific Ocean island nation.

Solidarity has meant listening to two young women exiled from their homeland in Eritrea, whose parents were leaders of the independence and resistance movements there and have since been held incommunicado as political prisoners. As they wrote "Free Oscar Now!" in their native Tigrinya, they reflected on the importance of people-to-people connections in building resistance across the planet among new generations of freedom fighters.

Any successful broad campaign must have goals and objectives that are clearly stated and adhered to, even if they are long-term in nature and even if, at first, it may seem—as it did to us in 1980—impossible that we would ever reach our goals. They must have unwavering principles, consistent and visible leadership, and an extremely flexible relationship between multiple strategies and tactics. There must be, at least over time, a sense of trust at the center, but also a sense of openness around the edges. Anyone must feel comfortable about joining no matter their experience level, political sophistication, belief system, or social background. Openness does not mean automatic equality between the people who have been part of the campaign for thirty years and those who joined yesterday. Communication, however, must be the key. At the center of the movement to free Oscar López Rivera, to free all Puerto Rican political prisoners, to free all U.S. political prisoners, there has not always been a sense of optimism. But there was never a sense of defeat. The motto "live and help to live" embodied our respect for one another and for "the people"—even at times of scorching disagreement or personal angst. We have been preparing for Oscar's release for literally thirty-five-plus years, and, as things got closer to when we felt the news would come, we tried to speak with "one voice for Oscar" in unity and strength.

Now that Oscar is free and can speak for himself, we reflect on the campaign not as victors but as ongoing organizers. We may take a moment here and there to sit back and celebrate, as we all deserve and need to do. But then, with the worst crisis in Puerto Rico's history, with confusion about what decolonization might look like at a time of global recolonization and rape of natural and human resources, with growing militarism and white supremacy and what sometimes looks like new forms of neoliberalism, we must continue and deepen our work in our communities. We must continue to empower our communities to name and solve their own problems. As Puerto Rican poet laureate and freedom fighter Juan Antonio Corretjer wrote, we must praise and glorify the hard work that builds up the people and the homeland: the human hands that can win over corporate greed.

From Charlottesville to North Korea, White Supremacy Feeds Endless War

On the weekend when Oscar López Rivera made his trium-phant and controversial first trip out of Puerto Rico to my hometown of New York City, the Fellowship of Reconciliation (FOR, the oldest ongoing peace group in the U.S.) held its National Council meeting in nearby Nyack. As an interfaith organization with deep roots in the "civil rights" movement and countless spiritually based human rights efforts, FOR was deeply supportive of the campaign for Oscar's freedom—but somehow managed anyway to elect me in absentia to serve as their national cochair. Sahar Alsahlani, who serves along with me, is a leader of the Council on American-Islamic Relations and was at the center of the religious convocation that took on the neo-Nazi organizing in Charlottesville, Virginia, in 2017. Following the violence and raw hatred sparked by the events in Charlottesville and subsequent cities, FOR issued the fol-lowing statement—penned by me and a handful of others—to make plain the connections between peace, justice, and the waves of racist violence we continue to face.

James Baldwin once wrote that America is a burning house, and now it seems the fire is spreading. The rage in the words and the fury in the eyes of those who proclaim that they intend to make America great again bring fear to the hearts of the rest of us. As hate-filled white supremacists spread their violence and rhetoric in Charlottesville, Virginia, and elsewhere, it seems as if our past failures have "come home to roost."

Both within and beyond the United States we are standing on the brink. Threats of violence being tossed back and forth between the governments of the U.S. and North Korea have taken us closer to absolute global disaster. President Trump tweeted: "Military Solutions are now fully in place, locked and loaded." The United States promised to deliver "fear and fury like the world has never seen." These words are reminiscent of the violent, incendiary language heard at the start of the last world war.

We refuse to learn lessons from previous generations. The defeated nations of World War II, Germany and Japan, were required by the Allies to include education for peace and human dignity in their constitutions. Yet the U.S. did not deem these lessons necessary for future generations of U.S. citizens. The result? The ideals of human rights and justice are lost to many who claim the U.S. as home.

But the promise of peace remains strong for many who work for a new world, emerging from the shell of the old. While both the U.S. and North Korean regimes have pushed the world yet closer to nuclear war, everyday people are looking for the security of fair housing, equitable education, freedom of expression, and freedom from both indirect and direct violence. Our needs include neither nuclear weapons nor militarized police.

Not all Republicans or Democrats may support the current plans for war, but their demonstrated bipartisan support for endless wars has paved the way to hatred, xenophobia, and separation. Funding for the weaponry of war goes largely unchallenged in the corridors of state power, despite claims that there aren't resources to help citizens on the margins fighting for survival or basic human needs. Tupac Shakur reminded us: "They got money for war, but can't feed the poor!"

In the tradition of the faithful in our struggle for peace and human dignity, we stand outraged at the buildup of arsenals that are turned on communities of color in the U.S. and globally. Instead of diplomacy and authentic humanitarian aid, the U.S. builds military bases abroad; rather than deal with the real economic issues of marginalized communities around our country, the U.S. hires thousands more police and militarizes them.

Communities of Indigenous, African, Latinx, and Asian descent, including immigrant communities of whatever legal status, seek economic and political refuge while being targeted by the very institutions they support in tax dollars. We believe security will only be possible when U.S. congressional leaders and the occupants of the White House respect the ideals and laws guaranteeing equal protection under the law, in areas of education, health care, access to the ballot, and more.

Lasting peace will only come with the presence of justice, which includes reparations and reconciliation: admitting, atoning, and paying for the crimes of past generations that remain unaccounted for. We must build an America of equality and peace that, in the prophetic words of Dr. Vincent Harding, "does not yet exist." Failing to condemn the racial hatred and murder we saw in Charlottesville and that we see as a consequence of wars only drives us in the opposite direction.

We must stop the current crash course toward disaster and take responsibility for all the disasters that have gone before, which the United States never has. Black Panther political prisoner Mumia Abu-Jamal recently stated, "White supremacy is the mother's milk of America," and the U.S. government needs to counter this demonstrated legacy by making amends to each and every community they have harmed. In the meantime, they have to *stop the war* on people abroad and domestically.

From Bayard Rustin, James Lawson, and Diane Nash to Vincent Harding, Ruby Sales, and many others, those representing the Fellowship of Reconciliation and our allies have worked to end war and to struggle for racial, economic, and all forms of justice. Rev. Dr. Martin Luther King, Jr., preached about all that was owed to oppressed communities in speaking of the "check marked insufficient funds." Later in King's life, he described the triple evils of militarism, materialism, and racism in U.S. life and developed a Poor People's Campaign, which is being resurrected today by current interfaith and community groups, including FOR.

The path forward must be supporting independent economic development in communities on the margins, rather than spending U.S. tax dollars on endless wars. In our time, we call for economic conversion, for money to support infrastructure that makes schooling equitable and empowering, for universal health care, for housing as a right that stems the tide of gentrification and gerrymandering, for the release of political prisoners and an end to mass incarceration, and for communities that place power in the hands of the people not the elite.

FOR calls the faithful to demand that the triplets of war, racism, and greed be challenged and consigned to the past. More than ever we must stand together for justice, to nonviolently challenge the endless war and racism we see both domestically and internationally. We cannot forget: we have the power!

In the struggle, Sahar Alsahlani, Anthony Grimes, Max Hess, Matt Meyer, David Ragland, and Ethan Vesely-Flad for the Fellowship of Reconciliation.

Extreme Solidarity

SNCC veteran and civil rights shero Ruby Sales reminds us that as we talk of peace and justice, we never develop a language that talks of social relations. We must not only speak truth to power but speak truth to one another. No one transcends the marks of our current crisis, Sales states, noting that the Rev. Dr. Martin Luther King, Jr. and Dr. Vincent Harding warned us that nothing short of a revolution of values would be needed to turn our society away from the deadly evils of materialism, militarism, and racism.

We can hardly deny that despite some positive reforms during the upsurge of Black liberation in the fifties, sixties, and seventies, many things are much, much worse today. And we can hardly deny that many in the USA seem to show significant love for Dr. King, our larger-than-life hero.

But we do little justice to our past legacies or to one another today when we forget that it was in a prison cell in Birmingham, Alabama, that Dr. King preached that we were—even then—well beyond reasonably asking whether or not we needed to take extreme measures to bring about freedom. The question Dr. King posed in his "Letter from Birmingham Jail" was: "What kind of extremists will we be?"

We have no right to go backward or stay stuck in one place, to squander the lessons or realities of the past, or to root ourselves in "same old, same old" methodologies, when it is clear that if we are serious about the gravity of our times, we must work harder to build our movements in more intense and serious fashions.

We must be extremists in our peace research. It is not sufficient, for example, for large numbers of people of European descent (aka "white folks") to attend a conference on justice and peace in the Deep South, on the theme of civil rights to human rights, and come knowing no more than a cursory amount about the Black-led freedom movements of the last half century. Yes, we know (as most elementary school children know) that drinking fountains for "colored" peoples were the norm in the Jim Crow South and that—from Colored to Negro to Black, Afro-American, African American, and beyond—mass movements emerged for basic citizenship rights.

But how many know the term "New Afrikan" and the struggle to "free the land" that still resonates in some circles, including among the base of supporters of the independent mayor of Jackson, Mississippi—Chokwe Antar Lumumba? I ask this not because I believe that we all have to agree with or even support the New Afrikan freedom movement, but because if we largely don't even know of its existence or basic history and positions—or of other traditions of Black history, from feminism to LGBT realities to so much more—then we enter into positions of potential solidarity largely ignorant, having ignored our basic "homework assignments." Just a few years ago, the idea that Bayard Rustin was both a leader of the 1963 March on Washington and also a gay man seemed to hit the progressive movement as a profound discovery, like Columbus discovering America. We have got to do better than that, got to do our homework and learn our lessons well and act more deeply like researchers so extremely and intensely in need of new ideas based on old truths, as if our lives depended on it. Because, in fact, they largely do.

The issue of the New Afrikan Independence Movement hit me on a personal level, because many years ago as a young organizer with the War Resisters League I noticed a group of folks who turned out to be New Afrikan adherents wearing buttons that simply read "At War." This seemed to me a curious reflection of the realities of the country I thought I was living in, before I understood that the U.S. was more of an empire, a prison house of occupied nations and territories and lands and peoples, than a typical nation-state. How shall we rectify the need for some folks to assert their resistance to war, while others need to proclaim their status as warriors in an ongoing conflict not of their making? We surely can't even begin to talk coalition politics if we don't even know of the existence of these positions.

Again, Ruby Sales has some poignant words of wisdom. At the 2017 Peace and Justice Studies Association conference held in none other than Birmingham, Sales stated that the USA was still "at war to preserve hegemony . . . with young people treated as enemy combatants." We are still in a civil war, a war in which "white America is faced with a spiritual crisis of identity, [with insatiable] greed, land theft, genocide, white patriarchal Christian imperialism . . . supporting a New World Order of capitalist technocracy." On the other side, suggests Sales, lie sites of isolation that will become Bantu communities like South Africa. We are, according to this lifelong movement veteran and visionary, sitting on a powder keg.

For me, it was nothing short of shocking to go from that conference to another in the center of Venezuela, where U.S. headlines would have one believe that civil war and economic chaos are about to break out. The grassroots systems of people-to-people bartering and sharing in place in the Indigenous and Afro-Venezuelan villages of that South American socialist experiment—"*trueke*" as they call it—mean that no one goes hungry or in need of shelter. There are divisions and disagreements, to be sure, but nothing on the scale of neo-Nazis running over peaceful antifascist church leaders and their supporters, as happened in Charlottesville, Virginia, at around the same time of these gatherings.

If we are to even come close to averting greater civil conflict in our own USA, to shielding ourselves from an explosion that will blow up in our own faces, we must become extremists in our pedagogy.

It is far from enough, at the end of the second decade of the twenty-first century, to accept any peace education that doesn't understand the dialectic and dialogical teachings of Paulo Freire, to deeply interrogate and overturn the power structures that exist in each of our classrooms and boardrooms, our study circles and conference panel discussions. Empowering students, workshop attendees, and community members to name their own world in order to better relate to it, those of us who are professors, teachers, administrators, facilitators, speechmakers, and leaders need to become students again, better students than before, listening more closely to those with less power and privilege and access and ease. When it comes to social change, we have much more to learn than to teach.

Rev. Osagyefo Sekou has told all those progressive professors who hold Ph.Ds to "get over yourselves" and get on with the work. Too often being an "academic and an activist" as is often claimed means being an academic who *talks about* activism or allows his students to do the same. It is time for teachers especially to walk the talk and understand the urgent need for action above words. The time for experts is over.

We must understand that the experiment called public education is coming to an end in the USA, and even a small pretense of mass education as a means to greater democracy is becoming shallower and hollower by the minute. If we look honestly at the data relating to quasi-clandestine, independent, deeply community-rooted Black education of the late slavery, Reconstruction, and Jim Crow eras, we'll find more examples of positive alternative practices for students of African descent than one can find today in our urban, factory-modeled, heavily centralized and standardized schools. A fully bipartisan campaign, sometimes callously calling itself the new civil rights movement, has come close to reaching its objective: to gain a substantial share of the trillion-dollar annual schools budget ($25 billion annually in New York City alone) in exchange for an entire generation or two being subject to crass experimentation under a system very likely to drive much of the creativity, individuality, sense of community, forward-thinking civics focus, and democracy itself out of our schools.

To even think about slowing this deadly process down within our own profession, we must become extremists about pedagogy and our practice.

We must become better organized, ready to build stronger organizations, practicing extreme honesty (and love) in calling one another out when we are dragging behind. In this age, for example, the task of transforming our world to one oriented toward peace can no longer be driven or led by small pockets of older white men, who hold the purse strings and call the shots. Our advisory boards, staff, memberships, and constituencies must reflect the science, wisdom, experience, and dreams of all the peoples surrounding us. This is not primarily a question of outreach; it is an age-old question of politics and economics, of institutional power in both our society and our movements. To truly move beyond the impasse we seem to face every few years—being on the verge of mass movements that then wane in the face of weak organization and consistency—we must not squander the opportunities we have when we come together at conferences or in the community.

Moving beyond war means moving beyond the violence, greed, and oppression at the root of all or most wars, energizing a new generation of leaders who will neither shy away from the task of highly disciplined, life-sacrificing work nor sell out to the highest bidder or the sexiest elder who seems to provide all the answers but rarely does much more than fly around the world giving only slightly modified versions of their well-polished rants.

We have, in moments of crisis, the opportunity to build new bridges of cooperation, collectivity, and coalition building, unleashing unprecedented levels of new excitement, new research, and a new and more diverse generation of comrades who will build deeper and denser networks of affinity: decentralized and willing to sacrifice and expect losses for the common good, able to build campaigns that will anticipate victories that we can celebrate.

When we embrace the need to take greater risks in these extremist times, to become more militant in our solidarity commitments to one another, we will surely have more allies than we could possibly imagine.

Looking at the White Left Historically

ONE MUST ADMIT THAT THERE HAVE BEEN TIMES IN THE struggle to survive the Trump presidency that things have gotten so negative one is tempted to write about the need to look *for*, not *at*, the idea of a U.S.-based "white" left.

When southern organizer Mandy Carter, Chicana historian Elizabeth "Betita" Martínez, and I came together to coedit the anthology *We Have Not Been Moved: Resisting Racism and Militarism in Twenty-First-Century America*, we did so with a cautious eye toward how we would define "whiteness" and the white left. We knew from that start that our basic thesis centered around the supposition that, despite many lessons to be learned from the movements of the fifties, sixties, and seventies, white progressives and radicals alike had largely not been moved by the experiences of their counterparts in the U.S. struggles of oppressed nationalities and peoples. This is not to say that racial identity—or any other individual "identity politics" configuration—sits comfortably with us in these twenty-first-century times. More and more (and perhaps most appropriately), lines of individual identity are blurred, as binaries and rigid self-definitions give way to multiple identity designations. As comedian Hari Kondabolu puts it, these days asking a white person their ethnic identity is like asking for a math equation with fractions. One-eighth German, one-sixteenth Saxon, one-third Cherokee, and so forth.

Defining what "the left" means in the U.S. (white, Black, or otherwise) is itself, at best, an inexact notion. There are enough Marxist, Maoist, Trotskyist, Democratic Socialist, anarchist, Gramscian, Green, and other formations that my partner has taken to calling them collectively the "wordy workers." Most of these groups, claiming to be the vanguard insofar as they have the answer to any question about "what is to be done" that one might care to ask, have members that span racial, ethnic, and cross-cultural categorization. But far too many also have a long and quite entrenched history of power brokers that come from communities of European descent. For all their radical ethics and theory, the practice of much of the formal U.S. left, from both diversity and effectiveness points of view, leaves a lot to be desired.

Beyond the left parties, party building structures, and pre-party formations, there is a growing mass of grassroots groupings, collectives, think tanks, and sometimes individuals with a history of working on a long list of causes, projects, and campaigns. It is hard not to note that even those that blossom into mass, national events or structures—from Occupy Wall Street to the Bernie Sanders electoral effort and beyond—tend to self-destruct along the fatal fault lines of not taking the "nonwhite world" seriously, respectfully, or even into account. We have not been moved by the simple but central truth that to undo the violence and injustices that surround us, we must get to the root of the problem. And the root of the problems facing the U.S. empire has everything to do with the stolen land, stolen labor, and colonized peoples who still bear the brunt of American exceptionalism and greed.

It is beyond the scope of this essay or even this book to give a full history of the U.S. left, white left, or even the white working class. But it is worth noting that—as celebrations of the fiftieth anniversary of the watershed year 1968 abound—a renewed interest in a reprinted booklet by a veteran of '68 has sparked some useful conversations. David Gilbert, a leading member of the Columbia University chapter of Students for a Democratic Society (SDS), put out—to much appropriate praise—his most comprehensive version of the now classic essay, "Looking at the U.S. White Working Class Historically."

Some background is needed.

David writes articulately in his excellent memoir *Love and Struggle* (PM Press, 2012) about his childhood growing up in Massachusetts, missing "the wink" that comes alongside stories of U.S. history that leave out the idea that "justice for all" never actually meant *all* the people living within the borders. He joined the social democratic SDS and was an early anti–Vietnam War activist and author of an influential SDS pamphlet naming imperialism as "the system" that the left was ostensibly up against. As a strong anti-imperialist, David participated in the 1968 Columbia student strike that shut down the university, making national and international headlines, as white and Black student radicals joined forces with Black community leaders in protesting Columbia's ever expanding gentrification policies that sought to take over much of West Harlem.

One has to appreciate historical context to make sense of what came next. In addition to the Columbia strike, 1968 was the year when the Vietnamese launched the successful Tet Offensive and when one U.S. military commander was famously quoted as saying, "We had to destroy that village in order to save it." It was the year the sitting U.S. president (who had taken the reins of power when JFK was killed) surprised the nation by declaring, amid ever growing national and regional demonstrations, that he "would not seek nor would he accept" nomination for reelection under his Democratic Party mantle. It was the year when "nonviolence died," with the assassinations of Robert Kennedy and Dr. Martin Luther King, Jr., the latter sparking rioting throughout the U.S. The Democratic Party's own national convention, held in Chicago with throngs of protests, including one organized by the newly formed Youth International Party (Yippies!), ended in a classic police riot that was broadcast widely on television screens across the world. It was the year when globally, revolution seemed both possible and likely, and—as beautifully chronicled in George Katsiaficas's *The Imagination of the New Left*—a new generation of radicals was coming into their own.

Revolution was in the air, and—to young radicals especially—it must have seemed like anything and everything could be accomplished with enough hard work.

Being part of an exclusive and disciplined group dedicated to "bringing the war home," therefore, must have seemed more rational at the time than 20/20 hindsight might suggest. For white students anxious to prove their seriousness compared to Black radicals calling out for actual power, the thought of going underground and considering clandestine options and direct violence against the state must have been more than plausible. After all, weren't escalating tactics called for as the U.S. became more militarized in both its foreign and domestic policies? Wasn't it appropriate to make the U.S. pay literally for their heinous acts, at the same time proving that the empire was not invincible and invulnerable? Wasn't it important to show that resistance and multifaceted struggle could continue despite the widespread repression that was being heaped upon radical movements, most especially the Black Panthers? David Gilbert, a former pacifist influenced by revolutionary nonviolence adherent Dave Dellinger, joined what would become the Weather Underground Organization (WUO), committed to blowing up buildings that symbolized U.S. government oppression. Even Dellinger agreed that being part of the WUO, which took great care not to harm or kill people in their actions, was preferable to watching on the sidelines (as so much of the white left did) as the FBI mercilessly attacked and murdered Black Panthers and the armed forces intensified their devastation of Southeast Asia.

In 1981, after more than a decade in hiding and short periods aboveground during which he helped develop an early chapter of a Men Against Sexism group and helped support grassroots, community-based education alternatives, David Gilbert was captured, charged, and convicted of felony murder, though there was and is no evidence that he was directly involved in anyone's death. Felony murder, which in 2018 again began to get widespread criticism from the legal and human rights communities, is the legal doctrine whereby anyone involved in an underlying felony (e.g., robbery) can be convicted with the full legal weight for any deaths that may result in an ensuing shoot-out (even if said person was not on the scene of the shoot-out at the time).

Despite deep self-criticisms and clearly declared remorse for the lives lost in the botched actions that led to his arrest, Gilbert remains in prison today, serving thirty-plus years of an interminable sentence that essentially acts as a slow-motion death penalty. Unless major changes take place in U.S. society—at very least major prison reforms—David will never again see the light of day in freedom.

Full disclosure necessitates that I divulge, as I write about the reprinting of his "Looking at the White Working Class Historically" essay (which I unabashedly paraphrased the title of): I am also a fan and a friend. My praise for him comes not based on his actions of the sixties or seventies, but on annual visits we have shared since the mid-eighties, as I have grown to appreciate his carefully considered thoughts about the nature of social change, his sly humor, his generous, loving spirit, his commitment to justice and liberation of all people, his openness to criticism and learning, and even his Bostonian pronunciations. David is one of the most profoundly antiracist white folks I have ever met (or heard about), and the hard time he does as a ward of the New York State Department of Corrections provides daily evidence of his ongoing service to the Black liberation movement and his revolutionary resolve. At any point in these decades, David could have eased his time and possibly even been released altogether—if only he had pointed a finger and said, "I didn't do anything. It was those guys who pulled the trigger and those other ones who pressured me to get involved in some crazy stuff."

There are ample parts of the white left in the U.S. who are satisfied with calling the WUO and its members nothing short of crazy. Some have, incredibly, likened them to mass murdering despots and petty dictators (perhaps mainly due to their admittedly authoritarian and sectarian practices); a few former members even ascribe the demise of the U.S. antiwar movement directly to the actions of Weather. I prefer to think that the real crazy is not to look at the Weather phenomenon in a dispassionate way, neither pumping them up as all horrible or super responsible but understanding the historical moment in which they emerged and operated.

On the other hand, as contemporary U.S. life and struggle get increasingly desperate, there are those who—in fairly uncritical ways—signify the Weather experiment as if it and its former leaders can provide the key answers to today's questions about strategy and tactics. There is a way in which *all* movement honchos of the 1960s seem to be seen by some as oracles of special knowledge about mass mobilization and revolution. Historical materialism and common sense combine to assert that movements ebb and flow based on particular economic, sociocultural, and political conditions—not because a single great man or woman make it so. It is nothing short of crazy, then, to continue to look for leadership from someone who made some provocative speeches between 1969 and 1972 during the height of an international upheaval, simply because they got their name in lights at a time when the mainstream media was more open and able to spotlight the left. After scores of book deals, college engagements, movies, manifestos, and more, if these folks alone had the essential answers about how to build an effective and lasting, diverse, and dynamic movement, we'd have had it by now.

We've got to find those answers collectively, in conversation with elders and youth and leaders past and present willing and able to engage in broad and honest dialogue. In my experience and that of many others, David Gilbert is an exemplary and fairly unique example of someone of his generation interested in just that type of collaborative, forward-looking connection.

Another aspect of full disclosure is this: in the aforementioned anthology *We Have Not Been Moved*, we reprinted in full an earlier version of David's "Looking at the White Working Class Historically" essay, because we agreed that it provided a vital analysis of the connections between race, class, and the role of U.S.-based white folks in building for lasting, positive change. It was therefore with some excitement that I learned of the plans to reprint it in an expanded, updated, contextualized format. And while it is unfair to review a volume that readers of this book don't have immediate access to, my own points of disappointment and chagrin regarding the latest version do provide some thoughts about solidarity, the white left, and moving forward that I believe to be instructive here.

Perhaps the area of greatest concern regarding David's new additions to his important prior writing center around a pandering to popular youthful notions about what we are currently up against. David correctly asserts that while it is necessary to be aware of the dire consequences of current affairs, we must remind ourselves that "the most basic issue is the very nature of the system."

David goes on to state:

> Nonetheless, there is something new and particularly threatening about Trump's election: the way he has enlarged, energized and emboldened an active and aggressive base for white supremacy. Immigrants, Muslims, Native American water protectors, Black Lives Matter activists, women who've faced sexual assault, LGBTQ folks, those who can't afford health insurance, and more all feel under the gun. The prospect of an unbridled pouring of more greenhouse gases into the atmosphere is terrifying. And there is a great danger he could provoke a major war, since in the past that has been the most effective way for unpopular presidents to rally public

> support behind them. We need much more of an
> anti-war movement.

There is nothing we would disagree with here. The problem is not in content or commission, it is one of emphasis and omission.

The nature of the integrated systems of imperialism and U.S.-centered racist, capitalist patriarchy very much hinges on the ways in which the U.S.—as much today as throughout history—serves as what has been termed a "prison house of nations." It is more vital than ever to emphasize that in looking at the countless laws, acts, statements, and policies of racist / sexist / homo- and transphobic and class-based content and intent, one cannot properly make sense of the whole without understanding that issues of individual or even community discrimination have little to do with the root of the problem. Intersectionality is a fine concept if we are mainly looking at the ways in which individuals are hurt and killed by "the system," but if we want to comprehend and build strategic campaigns and alliances against the system itself, we had better be sharper about our history. White supremacy and U.S. capitalist imperialism are based on the longtime takeover and control (land, labor, and more) of entire nations within and outside of our borders: Black (or African / New Afrikan from a revolutionary internationalist point of view), Puerto Rican, Mexican, and Indigenous (including Hawaiian and hundreds of Native nations).

This system continues to materially benefit all people of European descent and / or those who choose, consciously or otherwise (and those who simply accept, if only for a minute), the moniker of "white." Even for those seeking to be "race traitors," one cannot wave a private magic wand and personally step outside of centuries of psychological conditioning and social privilege, what it means to be brought up "white" in a society based on supremacist power. It thrives on traditional and new methods of colonialism, neocolonialism, mass imprisonment and repression, co-optation and criminalization of people's movements, economic and political disenfranchisement, devastation, and genocide. Trump's election and postelection policies are barely the tip of a very big iceberg.

When race and class oppression are reconfigured within an analysis that takes into account the long-term effects of settler colonialism, and the "internal" colonies of the Black nation, Native nations, Hawaii, and the northern half of Mexico are understood as much more than and different from simple oppressed "minorities," the significance of Puerto Rico—with its special insider / outsider status—comes into sharper view. Puerto Rico is seen by some as the Achilles heel of the U.S. empire; Puerto Ricans have the advantage of a clearly defined, ongoing, singular, and unifying land base, language, and culture, while experiencing the essential conditions of confinement and subjugation faced by the rest of the imperial subjects. For those shrewd Puerto Rican architects of effective movements and organizations, this duality of roles has enabled them to see the dialectics of change more clearly.

This is why David Gilbert's omission of the Puerto Rican–led and internationally recognized mass movements of the last decade is particularly glaring. While true that the Black Lives Matter actions and the mobilizations at Standing Rock were good signs of a reawakening population and communities of color–led initiatives that attracted some white support, there is evidence that the interrelated Puerto Rican campaigns have been built on firmer foundations. From the tactically diverse movement for Oscar López Rivera's freedom to the rallies and campaigns against the deeply recolonizing Puerto Rican economic debt management trap known as PROMESA, the Puerto Rican movement is not always as easily accessible or visible to the white left. But it is present nonetheless and has had consistent white allies working as part of and under the leadership of Puerto Rican organizations and individuals. The response to Hurricane Maria's intense effects on Puerto Rico reveals the ignorance and disconnect of parts of the U.S.-based white left, who spent weeks scrambling to figure out how best to help in non-paternalistic ways. It also reveals some strengths, as grassroots alternatives to the corporate hurricane relief efforts—which are more oriented toward providing relief to huge businesses than to the people in need—showcase deeply radical, off-the-radar work that has been slowly built up over decades. Thoughts about solar power in the mountains of Adjuntas, for example, came not from some clever gringo salesperson with solar panels to sell but from the same autonomous, antimining, ecological advocates who uncovered and fought successfully against environmentally and economically devastating Standard Oil plans close to forty years ago.

Subjective suggestions based on what friends are doing is fine but not enough. We must build comprehensive work based on more objective and thorough analysis of what feeds (and will thus starve) the empire.

Of course, there is much more that David Gilbert and I agree upon than not, and our central agreement still hinges on the idea that, as he puts it: "internationalism is not just a moral obligation . . . it is the only path to victory. The South is where consciousness and struggles tend to be the most advanced; that is what gives us a chance against this Goliath of a ruling class."

The lessons most needed now, the rules for twenty-first-century U.S. radicals, will mostly be found on the streets of Palestine, Egypt, and Tunisia; in the villages of Venezuela and the Maroon communities spread across South America and the Caribbean; in the reflections of the women of Mozambique and Sri Lanka; the conscientious objectors and war resisters of Korea and Eritrea; the Indigenous fighters around San Cristóbal de las Casas, Uluru, Pine Ridge and Standing Rock, Kashmir, Western Sahara, Vieques, and countless other locales. Closer to home, some lessons are available through careful listening to those with the most "advanced postdoctoral-level degrees" in resistance studies—research fellows at the University of Florence, Colorado (also known as the U.S. Penitentiary Administrative Maximum Facility), the College at Angola (aka the Louisiana State Penitentiary, appropriately built from and run like a slave plantation), and the Institute of Advanced Studies at Graterford, Pennsylvania (also known as the State Correctional Institution at Graterford). These are the types of places where Black Panthers like Sundiata Acoli, Imam Jamil Al-Amin (formerly known as H. Rap Brown), Mumia Abu-Jamal, Mutulu Shakur, and Russell Maroon Shoatz were or are still held, where American Indian Movement leader Leonard Peltier languishes despite mountains of evidence of his innocence, where members of the MOVE 9 remain incarcerated for refusing to conform to a lifestyle complicit with inner city genocidal neighborhood policies, and where David Gilbert lives out his life.

One does not have to agree with everything all of these people have done or continue to say. But one absolutely has to deeply understand and take into account their experiences with the current conditions of empire—to know the hidden histories so often obscured from mass view. Looking historically and particularly at the U.S.-based white left, we have not been nearly good enough listeners and have barely even sought out the collective lessons of struggle from those at the front lines in the confrontation with empire. Beyond listening, we are in dire need of processing these lessons and figuring out concrete solidarity actions that can propel all movements forward.

We may work to free U.S.-based political prisoners because they have worked to liberate their own people and others; we may work to free them because they inspire us or teach us. But we may also want to free them because on basic humanitarian levels, it is time—after scores of decades—to end the torture and bring them home. Beyond all this, however, all progressives should want to free them because no movement that will be taken seriously in the future allows its members to be repressed without consequence. No serious movement sits idly by watching their elders die behind bars. We must work to free the U.S. political prisoners in order to free ourselves.

Similarly, we may work in solidarity with the peoples of the Global South because we know in the U.S. and elsewhere in the North, we have access to resources that can do extraordinary good. We may work or make contributions as a form of reparations, owed many times over based on past and ongoing theft of land, labor, natural resources, and more. Reparations must be a vital part of our twenty-first-century movements. But, beyond this, we should work with our counterparts in Africa, Asia and the Pacific, South America and the Caribbean, because many movements there are so much further advanced in their praxis, with creative, forceful processes for delinking from oppressive global systems. Many have long moved beyond the myths and false dichotomies still prevalent in the U.S. left. In many ways the white left here is the true "undeveloped country," complete with infantile tendencies and stunted growth based on centuries inside of a reactionary cauldron, the pressure cooker (not melting pot) of U.S. society.

If we are to get to a point where white lives no longer matter more than other lives, it will be because enough of us have confronted our history and our contemporary conditions with intensity, honesty, and a nonsectarian approach to all those who fight for freedom and liberation in various forms. It will be because we ourselves have confronted those in our communities and country who vehemently disagree with us—who want to bring us to an ever whiter time where, honestly, "being great" means an end to democracy and even a hint of justice for all. It will be because we are embracing and not exclusionary in our approaches, sharply critical but not criticizing in our analysis, confrontational and militant but not authoritarian or militaristic in our operations. We can build unity without mandating unanimity and incorporate many truths and experiments with truth into our agendas. We can and must be both revolutionary and loving.

For all who agree that white lives shouldn't matter most, there is much work to be done.

There are more than one or two ways to move forward and begin, continue, or increase the work.

But the time to start is now.

CONCLUSION
REMOVING OUR WHITE-COLORED GLASSES—
FACING REALITY AND FIGHTING AGAINST EMPIRE

ONCE UPON A TIME, ABOUT A HUNDRED YEARS AGO, THERE was a smallish peace movement and a rather largish war, called by most "the war to end all wars." It certainly did not live up to its catchphrase hype. Less than one generation later, an even larger war—one of the biggest the world had ever seen—spread throughout the lands. Because most of it was fought in Europe, it was called a World War and, in deference to the one before, was given the number two. That one, many people said, was a good one: after all, capitalists and communists were fighting together, and Blacks and whites were fighting together, and even the women were encouraged to say "Yay" and support the war effort both at home and in the factories. Only a few crazy pacifists suggested that there were better ways to fight Nazism and fascism than through militarism and war, but even Gandhi said it was okay for Indian soldiers to be conscripted into British regiments to fight the Germans, Italians, and Japanese. Later, in the USA (which was happily and well on its way to becoming a leading imperial power), some pointed out what peace leader A.J. Muste said: "There is no way to peace; peace is the way." But he was probably quoting someone else.

Once upon a time, about fifty years ago, there was a huge peace movement against a war in a rather smallish place. This time, the capitalists and the communists were really going at it against one another, and the poorest people furthest away from the centers of power were being killed at extraordinary rates by both extraordinary and ordinary weapons. Even without the internet, alliances built up between people from one corner of the planet to another, and people of African descent at the center of empire (noting that no one of Asian descent from where the war was taking place had ever called them bad names) raised the cry: "Hell No, We Won't Go." We won't fight wars that are not to anyone's but the capitalists' and imperialists' benefit. So Stokely Carmichael and Ella Baker, Fannie Lou Hamer and Malcolm X, and Martin Luther King, Jr., at the very end of his life, all helped make clear that resisting war, abolishing war—going "beyond Vietnam," as Dr. King and Dr. Vincent Harding spoke of, or "beyond war"—was a vital concern and priority for all the peoples of the world. The narrow, single-issue advocates ("end only the most overt aspects of this one specific war") ended up being led by diverse coalitions of peoples who generally agreed that all or at least most war and the causes of war itself had to be fully abolished in order for the planet and its people to thrive.

This is the sixties and seventies legacy so often searched for. Neither the cleverness of the organizers of that period nor the enormity of the mobilizations make up the true "lessons of the sixties." They weren't nearly as clever as they thought they were, and the demonstrations weren't nearly as large as the ones that came in the decades to follow. The historic and material conditions of that era led the world (and the North American part of it) to be drawn into a radical spirit of possibility and hope. The ability to dream big, to confront the nightmares boldly, and to struggle together for deeper unity amidst diversity was the clearest lesson. This twenty-first-century moment, looking toward the third decade of this century, is on the precipice of taking that lesson to heart.

We are poised to forge the radical essence of justice into the wide-ranging vision of lasting peace.

Once upon a time, as the empire was beginning to crumble, some of the older peace and justice organizations from every faith background and from the secular political left began to take heed of these histories and to change. "Feminism" may still have been a contentious word, but it was clear that women had to take the lead. "People of color" was another contentious term, but the people it sought to describe were taking leadership roles in new and challenging ways. Some new organizations emerged, dedicated to more intersectional perspectives; other new organizations emerged, dedicated to replicating the narrow, more segregated organizing modes of the past. With rabid imperial dogs lashing out, it was hard to see sharply enough to go forward.

We must now be prepared to remove our white-colored glasses and to look at the world beyond anything the U.S. left has yet begun to contemplate.

Reparations: The Thin Black Line between White and Woke

One step in new thinking and rebuilding must be taken internally, through individual reflection on our identities, complicities, and roles. Identity politics itself can never go beyond liberal tokenism but must be understood to develop structural and personal accountability within our movements.

The following reflection was shared in the midst of a particularly difficult real-life conflict in an organization struggling to transform itself:

In thinking about myself at this moment in U.S. history, it would be foolish not to recognize and overtly acknowledge the power and privilege I have as someone born and raised white and male in the late twentieth century. While I do not believe that biology is destiny and am acutely aware that people of my ethnic / racial / cultural / religious background were not considered "white" in many parts of the world less than a century ago, I am also absolutely clear that in contemporary U.S. society, "whiteness" is a construct that has been bestowed on people of my background and utilized here and elsewhere to oppress others. For almost my entire adult life, I have been a proponent of the concept that *all* white folks raised in a racist, imperialist, colonizing society such as ours are inevitably also racist, carrying within us the self-righteous and self-serving seeds of oppressive behaviors—behaviors that have to be struggled and fought against in many forms over our entire lifetimes. There are, in my opinion and experience, a number of good white folks struggling for decades in solidarity with movements and peoples working for their own liberation, but there are absolutely no "special white folks" exempt from the need for constant, ongoing, personal, and institutional work. No white person becomes "an antiracist" and gets to sit on his or her laurels or past history or imagined "race traitor" politics and get a pass from engaging in the work.

Given this position, and my commitment to working to push forward this work and politics, I find it impossible now not to take public responsibility for any part I might have played or harm I might have caused due to my identity and privilege. As we, all of us, become more aware and conscious of the realities and effects of microaggression and trauma, it is the responsibility of those of us with the most opportunity to exert undue and oppressive power to listen most carefully and be held accountable to those who in this society have been most oppressed. As we build collective struggle and practice within our organization against patriarchy, white supremacy, and other forms of oppression, I not only want to be accountable to whatever structures and processes we have or may set up to monitor this but also pledge to be mindful and accountable to any individuals who have felt or feel harmed. I am thus open to any forms of interpersonal mediation that seem warranted, desired, or helpful.

Radicalism requires us to not elevate identity politics to a reactive state. Accusations cannot be automatic judgments, and an individual's feelings, no matter how heartfelt, cannot automatically be evaluated to a position of ultimate truth (though they can be understood contextually as part of the truth). No punishment or adverse consequences should result from the rendering of unsubstantiated charges. To do so would undermine any sense of internal justice or fairness and undermine any attempt at true institutional or individual change, beyond an identity / nationalist determinism. But we must, as Amber McZeal asserts, struggle most intensely to "decolonize the psyche"—and that process within the organization must start, for each of us, within ourselves.

Reparations—the personal, political, institutional, and fiscal responsibilities of all people born of privilege to help repair the ongoing harm done and equalize our power dynamics—are a key first step to being "woke" in these especially dangerous times.

Next Steps and New Horizons

In contemplating white lives in modern USA and looking for philosophical guideposts for revolutionary next steps, I find it useful to look back a bit to the mature perspectives of Dr. Martin Luther King, Jr. He wrote, in a little known 1966 speech called "Don't Sleep through the Revolution," the following reflection:

> One of the great misfortunes of history is that all too many individuals and institutions find themselves in a great period of change and yet fail to achieve the new attitudes and outlooks that the new situation demands. There is nothing more tragic than to sleep through a revolution. . . . Most revolutions in the past have been based on hope and hate, with the rising expectations of the revolutionaries implemented by hate for the perpetrators of the unjust system in the old order. I think the different thing about the revolution that has taken place in [the USA during the "civil rights" era] is that it has maintained the hope element and at the same time it has added the dimension of love.

In King's more popular 1967 speech "Where Do We Go from Here?" he continued his treatise on revolution and love-force, dealing head-on with the question of the proper use of power. He wrote:

What is needed is a realization that power without love is reckless and abusive, and that love without power is sentimental and anemic. Power at its best is love implementing the demands of justice, and justice at its best is love correcting everything that stands against love. . . . This is no time for romantic illusions and empty philosophical debates about freedom. This is a time for action. What is needed is a strategy for change, a tactical program.

Though quoting King and admiring his work from afar is one of the most common pitfalls of the contemporary white apologist for the status quo, somehow King's more radical views are consistently absent from their citations. In the fifty years since King's assassination, many strategies and tactics have been developed for the moral, political, and economic revival needed to resuscitate a true people's movement in the belly of the imperial beast. And movement building is not a tangential part of the work for justice and freedom. As the great organizer, teacher, and author Vincent Harding (who penned with Martin Luther King the 1967 "Beyond Vietnam" speech) once noted: it is the movement itself that helps us become truly human.

Some campaigns and initiatives of the last three decades have been more successful than others; none of these has been adequately studied and examined by most movement academics or organizers, who prefer instead to dwell on older battles and more tried and true (and largely unsuccessful) past strategies and tactics. Campaigns for national electoral change, rallies that have people standing listening for hours to similar speeches, marches with little specific target or goal— all of these may feel good for a moment, or even succeed in a limited manner. But without an overarching strategic focus and campaign plan none of these methods will build new movements or alter long-term social dynamics.

The empire, however, will die. Parts of the planet, and many, many people and species, will likely die with it.

But If the planet survives, it seems also likely that whiteness will carry on. White supremacy is too important a centerpiece of fascist, and / or neo-imperial, and / or multi-national capitalist barbarism.

The urgent question we must now ask ourselves, our organizations, and our movements is: What matters most as we build for something new?

About the Authors

Matt Meyer is an internationally recognized author, academic, organizer, and educator who currently serves as national co-chair of the Fellowship of Reconciliation, the oldest interfaith peace and justice group in the U.S. As former national chair of the War Resisters League, he is only the second person to be elected to the top position of both historic organizations, following A.J. Muste—"dean of the U.S. peace movement." Based in New York City, Meyer has led seminars, trainings, and conferences in over sixty countries on five continents. He is the United Nations representative for the International Peace Research Association and sits on the executive committee of that organization. He is also the Africa Support Network coordinator for War Resisters' International and a member of the financial advisory committee of the International Fellowship of Reconciliation. In 2018, Meyer was appointed senior research scholar of the University of Massachusetts / Amherst Resistance Studies Initiative. Argentine Nobel Peace laureate Adolfo Pérez Esquivel, who wrote the introduction to Meyer's encyclopedic anthology on contemporary movements to free political prisoners, *Let Freedom Ring* (PM Press, 2008), noted that "Meyer is a coalition-builder," one who "provides tools for today's activists" in his writings and his work. For over thirty years, Meyer worked to build alternative education structures within the New York City Department of Education, serving as the Alternative School's multicultural coordinator under three superintendents. Meyer serves as a board member of the A.J. Muste Memorial Institute and is an editorial board member of the peer-reviewed *Peace and Change*, co-published by the Peace History Society and the Peace and Justice Studies Association, of which he was founding co-chairperson. He is part of the Resistance in Brooklyn (RnB) collective, working on issues of Puerto Rican solidarity, dismantling the prison and military industrial complexes, and community empowerment. He is contributor to and co-editor with dequi kioni-sadiki of *Look for Me in the Whirlwind: From the Panther 21 to 21st Century Revolutions* (PM Press, 2017), which *Publisher's Weekly* gave a starred review. Along with Elizabeth "Betita" Martinez and Mandy Carter, Meyer co-edited and wrote *We Have Not Been Moved: Resisting Racism and Militarism in 21st Century America* (PM Press, 2012), which Maya Angelou noted was "so needed" for its "investigation of the moral issues of our time." In the foreword to Meyer's first book, *Guns and Gandhi in Africa: Pan African Insights on Nonviolence, Armed Struggle and Liberation* (Africa World Press, 2000), co-authored with Bill Sutherland, Archbishop Desmond Tutu wrote that Sutherland and Meyer "have looked beyond the short-term strategies and tactics which too often divide progressive peoples. . . . They have begun to develop a language which looks at the roots of our humanness."

Sonia Sanchez: Poet. Mother. Professor. National and international lecturer on Black culture and literature, women's liberation, peace, and racial justice. Sponsor of Women's International League for Peace and Freedom. Board member of MADRE. Sonia Sanchez is the author of over twenty books including *Homecoming, We a BaddDDD People, Love Poems, I've Been a Woman, A Sound Investment and Other*

Stories, Homegirls and Handgrenades, Under a Soprano Sky, Wounded in the House of a Friend (Beacon Press, 1995), *Does Your House Have Lions?* (Beacon Press, 1997), *Like the Singing Coming Off the Drums* (Beacon Press, 1998), *Shake Loose My Skin* (Beacon Press, 1999), and most recently *Morning Haiku* (Beacon Press, 2010). In addition to being a contributing editor to *Black Scholar* and *The Journal of African Studies*, she edited the anthology, *We Be Word Sorcerers: 25 Stories by Black Americans. BMA: The Sonia Sanchez Literary Review*, the first African American journal to discuss the work of Sonia Sanchez and the Black Arts Movement. A recipient of a National Endowment for the Arts, the Lucretia Mott Award for 1984, the Outstanding Arts Award from the Pennsylvania chapter of the National Coalition of 100 Black Women, the Community Service Award from the National Black Caucus of State Legislators, she is also a winner of the 1985 American Book Award for *Homegirls and Handgrenades*, the Governor's Award for Excellence in the Humanities for 1988, the Peace and Freedom Award from Women International League for Peace and Freedom (WILPF) for 1989, a PEW Fellowship in the Arts for 1992–1993 and the recipient of Langston Hughes Poetry Award for 1999. *Does Your House Have Lions?* was a finalist for the National Book Critics Circle Award. She is the Poetry Society of America's 2001 Robert Frost Medalist and a Ford Freedom Scholar from the Charles H. Wright Museum of African American History. Her poetry also appeared in the movie *Love Jones*. Sonia Sanchez has lectured at over five hundred universities and colleges in the United States and has traveled extensively, reading her poetry in Africa, Cuba, England, the Caribbean, Australia, Europe, Nicaragua, the People's Republic of China, Norway, and Canada. She was the first Presidential Fellow at Temple University, and she held the Laura Carnell Chair in English at Temple University. She is the recipient of the Harper Lee Award, 2004, Alabama Distinguished Writer, and the National Visionary Leadership Award for 2006, as well as the 2005 Leeway Foundation Transformational Award and the 2009 Robert Creeley Award. Currently, Sonia Sanchez is one of twenty African American women featured in "Freedom Sisters," an interactive traveling exhibition created by the Cincinnati Museum Center and Smithsonian Institution. In December of 2011, Philadelphia Mayor Michael Nutter selected Sonia Sanchez as Philadelphia's first Poet Laureate, calling her "the longtime conscience of the city." *BaddDDD Sonia Sanchez*, a documentary about Sanchez's life as an artist and activist by Barbara Attie, Janet Goldwater, and Sabrina Schmidt Gordon was nominated for a 2017 Emmy. She also provided the after-poem to Matt Meyer, Elizabeth "Betita" Martinez, and Mandy Carter's co-edited anthology *We Have Not Been Moved: Resisting Racism and Militarism in 21stCentury America* (PM Press, 2012).

The **Fellowship of Reconciliation** is the oldest interfaith peace and justice group in the U.S. When we wrote our collective 2018 statement, Sahar Alsahlani, Anthony Grimes, Max Hess, Matt Meyer, David Ragland, and Ethan Vesely-Flad were all national FOR leaders of staff or council.

Fred Ho (1957–2014), saxophonist, composer, and revolutionary Marxist, was a dynamic and prolific force within jazz and radical left movements for over forty years. A baritone saxophonist inspired by the avant-garde currents in African, Asian, and diasporic music, Ho despised the term "Jazz," considering it an insulting term for a powerful tradition. As a Marxist, Ho embraced and drew inspiration from the revolutionary movements against colonialism that swept the world in the 1960s and 1970s, from Vietnam to the U.S. Black

Liberation Movement. He brought explicitly socialist and radical left politics to his performances like no other working musician during his wide-ranging music career, which formally began in 1985 with the LP *Tomorrow Is Now* (Soul Note). Towards the end of his life, he formed Scientific Soul Sessions to intensify and fuse his cultural, political, and philosophical visions and programs and dedicated himself to working for the freedom of incarcerated Black liberation leader Russell "Maroon" Shoatz, to the creation of an eco-socialist program for planetary survival, to the a revitalization of a new Black arts movements, to battling cancer and all the toxins of capitalism, and to struggling to develop a politics of revolutionary indigeneity, radical matriarchy, and anti-imperialism.

Natalie Jeffers, a specialist in communications and the repurposing of research for new and non-academic audiences, is founder / director of Matters of the Earth.

Ana López is a professor at Hostos Community College in the Bronx, New York, and served as the New York City coordinator of the Campaign to Free Oscar López Rivera. A lifelong revolutionary Puerto Rican independence activist, López is co-editor of Oscar López Rivera's book of correspondence with his granddaughter, *Letters to Karina* (2016).

David Ragland is Senior Bayard Rustin Fellow at the Fellowship of Reconciliation, co-founder and former co-director of the Truth Telling Project of Ferguson, Missouri, and a visiting professor at Pacifica Graduate Institute in Community Liberation and Eco-Psychology. David is a regular contributor to the *Huffington Post* and *PeaceVoice*; his writings can also be found in *YES! Magazine*, *Waging Nonviolence*, *CounterPunch*, and in the forthcoming *Peace Studies Between Tradition and Innovation*.

Index

"Passim" (literally "scattered") indicates intermittent discussion of a topic over a cluster of pages.

Abu-Jamal, Mumia, 69, 88
Ainu, 33
Alexander, Michelle, 14
All-African People's Revolutionary Party (AAPRP), 41, 44–45
Alsahlani, Sahar: "From Charlottesville to North Korea, White Supremacy Feeds Endless War," 67–70
American Friends Service Committee, 46
American Indians. See Native Americans
"antiracist whites," 27–28, 39
antiwar movements. See peace movements
armed struggle, 8, 21, 46, 47, 51

Baker, Ella, 6, 92
Baldwin, James, 31–32, 33, 36, 67
Barson, Ben, 31–33
Bayard, Clare, 12
Black Lives Matter, 4, 18, 21, 39, 81, 86
Black Panther Party, 11, 15, 21, 43, 69, 88
Black Power movement, 6, 41, 42
Braden, Anne, 5, 11

Brown, Bob, 41–45 passim
Brown, John, 11

Cabeza de Vaca, Alvar Núñez, 35
Cabral, Amílcar, 50–51
Cagan, Leslie, 41–44 passim
campaign organizing. See organizing
Carmichael, Stokely. See Ture, Kwame (Stokely Carmichael)
Cartas a Karina (López Rivera), 54
Carter, Mandy: We Have Not Been Moved, 77, 83–84
Casas, Bartolomé de las, 35
Charlottesville, Virginia, 67–68, 69, 74
Chicago, 53, 60, 80
Christianity, 35, 73. See also Quakers
civil disobedience, 61
class, 48, 83–86 passim
Clinton, Bill, 61
COINTELPRO, 21, 40
colonialism, 86. See also decolonization
Columbia University student strike, 1968, 79
Cone, James, 23
Corretjer, Juan Antonio, 66

decolonization, 65; mental, 95; Puerto Rico, 55, 63, 65, 66. *See also* United Nations Special Committee on Decolonization

Dellinger, David, 81

Deming, Barbara, 49–50

Democratic National Convention, Chicago, 1968, 80

demonstrations, protests, etc., 43, 55, 80, 92

Diego Garcia, 65

Diener, Sam, 34–35

direct action, 61–62

Du Bois, W.E.B., 2–3, 5

East Timor, 65

Ecosocialist Horizons, 26

education, public. *See* public education

egotism, 28–29

elected officials, 59–61 passim, 69. *See also* Obama, Barack

ends and means, 50

Eritrea, 65

Evans, Sara: *Free Spaces*, 34–35

Fanon, Frantz, 49–50

FBI, 21, 40, 81

Fellowship of Reconciliation, 67–70

felony murder, 81

firearms. *See* guns

Free Spaces: The Sources of Democratic Change in America (Evans), 34–35

Freire, Paulo, 25

Fuerzas Armadas de Liberación Nacional Puertorriqueña (FALN), 54

Gandhi, Mohandas, 49, 64, 91

Gilbert, David, 11, 39, 79–88 passim

Grimes, Anthony: "From Charlottesville to North Korea, White Supremacy Feeds Endless War," 67–70

Guevara, Che, 49

guns, 13, 15, 43. *See also* armed struggle

Gutiérrez, Luis, 59, 60

Harding, Vincent, 43, 69, 71, 92, 97

"Hell No, We Won't Go!," 42, 92

Hess, Max: "From Charlottesville to North Korea, White Supremacy Feeds Endless War," 67–70

Ho, Fred: "Toward a Maroon Society: Working Together to Build a New World," 26–40

identity politics, 77, 93, 95

The Imagination of the New Left (Katsiaficas), 80

imprisonment. *See* prisons and imprisonment

Indigenous Americans. *See* Native Americans

Jeffers, Natalie: "If Mental Illness Is the Problem, America Is Mentally Ill," 13–16; "Refusing to Choose between Malcolm and Martin," 17–25

Jegroo, Ashoka, 23

Johnson, Lyndon, 79–80

Joseph, Gloria, 5

Katsiaficas, George: *Imagination of the New Left*, 80
King, Martin Luther, Jr., 13, 16–23 passim, 42–43, 46, 49, 70, 71, 96–97; assassination, 80; Vietnam War, 22, 42–43, 92
Kondabolu, Hari, 77
Kouyate, Mawina Sowa, 41, 45

Lance, Mark, 33–34
Las Casas, Bartolomé de. *See* Casas, Bartolomé de las
lawn signs, 10–11
left, U.S. *See* U.S. left
left, white. *See* white left
Look for Me in the Whirlwind: From the Panther 21 to 21st-Century Revolutions, 1
"Looking at the White Working Class Historically" (Gilbert), 79, 82–86 passim
López, Ana: "Oscar López Rivera," 52–66
López, José E., 53, 58
López Rivera, Oscar, 52–67 passim, 86
Lorde, Audre, 5, 25
love and power. *See* power and love
Love and Struggle (Gilbert), 79
Lumumba, Chokwe Antar, 72

Machel, Samora, 51
Malcolm X, 11, 19–23 passim, 43, 46, 92
Mandela, Nelson, 53, 54
March on Washington for Jobs and Freedom, 1963, 22, 72
Mark-Viverito, Melissa, 59, 60
"Maroon whites," 29–31, 34, 38

Maroons, 26–40 passim
Martínez, Elizabeth: *We Have Not Been Moved*, 77, 83–84
mass shootings, 13, 16
matriarchy, 30, 31, 36
Mauritius, 65
McZeal, Amber, 95
means and ends. *See* ends and means
media, 59, 60, 83
mental illness, 13–14
Merrymount Community, Massachusetts Colony, 35
militarism, 50–51, 68–70 passim, 80
Mobilization for Survival, 41, 44–45
Morton, Thomas, 35
Muste, A.J., 91
Muthien, Bernadette, 40
The Mythology of the White Proletariat from Mayflower to Modern (Sakai), 2

National Rifle Association (NRA), 13, 14
Native Americans, 87, 88
Navy, U.S. *See* U.S. Navy
New Afrikan Independence Movement, 72, 73
New York Free Oscar Coordination Group, 59
Nicaragua, 64–65
Nieves Falcón, Luis, 58
nonviolence, 8, 21, 24, 43, 46–50 passim, 61
North Korea, 68
Núñez Cabeza de Vaca, Alvar. *See* Cabeza de Vaca, Alvar Núñez

Obama, Barack, 55
Odinga, Sekou, 11, 39–40
"On Being White . . . and Other Lies" (Baldwin), 31–32
Organization of American States, 53
organizing, ix, 4–12 passim, 57–63 passim

Pan-Africanism, 42, 45
pardons, presidential. See presidential pardons and commutations
passivity, 8, 49, 50
paternalism, 6, 7, 46, 87
peace movements, 41–46 passim, 91–93
police, 4, 16, 17, 69
political organizing. See organizing
political prisoners, 26, 27, 37–38, 52–66 passim, 81–89 passim
politicians, elected. See elected officials
power and love, 96–97
presidential pardons and commutations, 61
prisons and imprisonment, 9, 10, 17, 88. See also political prisoners
Progressive Student Network, 42
protests, demonstrations, etc. See demonstrations, protests, etc.
public education, 75
Puerto Rico, 52–66 passim, 86–87

Quakers, 11, 46

Ragland, David: "From Charlottesville to North Korea, White Supremacy Feeds Endless War," 67–70; "If Mental Illness Is the Problem, America Is Mentally Ill," 13–16; "Refusing to Choose between Malcolm and Martin," 17–25
Ramos-Horta, José, 65
"rematriation," 40
reparations, 23, 96
Rustin, Bayard, 72

Sakai, J.: Mythology of the White Proletariat from Mayflower to Modern, 2
Sales, Ruby, 71, 73
Sanchez, Sonia, ix–xi
schools and schooling, 75
Scientific Soul Sessions (SSS), 26, 37
Scott, Imani Michelle, 16
SDS. See Students for a Democratic Society (SDS)
Second Amendment, 15
Sekou, Osagyefo, 5, 74
self-defense, 19, 43, 50
sentencing, punitive, 54
Shakur, Assata, 21, 22
Shakur, Tupac, 69
Shoatz, Russell Maroon, 26, 27, 37–38, 88
Shoatz, Theresa, 37
shootings, mass. See mass shootings
Showing Up for Racial Justice (SURJ), 5
SNCC. See Student Nonviolent Coordinating Committee (SNCC)

social class. *See* class
Society of Friends. *See* Quakers
solidarity, 39, 46–52 passim,
    72, 76, 89, 94; with political
    prisoners, 38, 62–65 passim
standardized tests, 10
Standing Rock Indian Reserva-
    tion, 86
Student Nonviolent Coordinating
    Committee (SNCC), 6–7, 44
Students for a Democratic
    Society (SDS), 79
Sutherland, Bill, 45, 46

tests, standardized. *See* stan-
    dardized tests
Trump, Donald, 68, 84, 86
Tubman, Harriet, 11
Ture, Kwame (Stokely Carmi-
    chael), 6, 7–8, 24–25, 41–45
    passim, 92
Tutu, Desmond, 53, 64

United Nations Special Com-
    mittee on Decolonization,
    55, 64
U.S. left, 78
U.S. Navy, 65
U.S. Student Association, 43

Venezuela, 73–74
Vesely-Flad, Ethan: "From
    Charlottesville to North
    Korea, White Supremacy
    Feeds Endless War," 67–70
Vietnam War, 53, 79–80, 81,
    91–92; antiwar movement, 44,
    79; MLK and, 22, 42–43, 92
violence, 13–18 passim, 25, 50,
    51, 67–69 passim. *See also*
    war and wars

war and wars, 68–70, 76, 91–92.
    See also Vietnam War
War Resisters' International, 46
War Resisters League, 73
*We Have Not Been Moved:
    Resisting Racism and Milita-
    rism in Twenty-First-Century
    America* (Martinez, Meyer,
    and Carter), 77, 83–84
Weather Underground Organi-
    zation (WUO), 81, 82, 83
Western Massachusetts, 5
White House civil disobedience
    actions, 61
white left, 77–90 passim
whiteness, 27, 30–36 passim,
    77, 94, 98
white privilege, 28, 94–95
whites, antiracist. *See* "antiracist
    whites"
whites, Maroon. See "Maroon
    whites"
whites and SNCC, 6–7, 44
Women for Oscar, 63
World War I, 91
World War II, 68, 91

X, Malcolm. *See* Malcolm X

Yulín, Carmen, 59

Zinn, Howard, 2

WE HAVE NOT BEEN MOVED
Resisting Racism and Militarism in 21st Century America
Edited by Elizabeth Betita Martínez, Mandy Carter, and Matt Meyer
Introduction by Cornel West
Afterwords/poems by Alice Walker and Sonia Sanchez
$29.95
ISBN: 978-1-60486-480-9
6x9 • 608 pages

We Have Not Been Moved is a compendium addressing the two leading pillars of U.S. Empire. Inspired by the work of Dr. Martin Luther King Jr., who called for a "true revolution of values" against the racism, militarism, and materialism which he saw as the heart of a society "approaching spiritual death," this book recognizes that—for the most part—the traditional peace movement has not been moved far beyond the half-century-old call for a deepening critique of its own prejudices. While reviewing the major points of intersection between white supremacy and the war machine through both historic and contemporary articles from a diverse range of scholars and activists, the editors emphasize what needs to be done now to move forward for lasting social change. Produced in collaboration with the War Resisters League, the book also examines the strategic possibilities of radical transformation through revolutionary nonviolence.

Among the historic texts included are rarely-seen writings by antiracist icons such as Anne Braden, Barbara Deming, and Audre Lorde, as well as a dialogue between Dr. King, revolutionary nationalist Robert F. Williams, Dave Dellinger, and Dorothy Day. Never-before-published pieces appear from civil rights and gay rights organizer Bayard Rustin and from celebrated U.S. pacifist supporter of Puerto Rican sovereignty Ruth Reynolds. Additional articles making their debut in this collection include new essays by and interviews with Fred Ho, Jose Lopez, Joel Kovel, Francesca Fiorentini and Clare Bayard, David McReynolds, Greg Payton, Gwendolyn Zoharah Simmons, Ellen Barfield, Jon Cohen, Suzanne Ross, Sachio Ko-Yin, Edward Hasbrouck, Dean Johnson, and Dan Berger. Other contributions include work by Andrea Dworkin, Mumia Abu-Jamal, Starhawk, Andrea Smith, John Stoltenberg, Vincent Harding, Liz McAlister, Victor Lewis, Matthew Lyons, Tim Wise, Dorothy Cotton, Ruth Wilson Gilmore, Kenyon Farrow, Frida Berrigan, David Gilbert, Chris Crass, and many others. Peppered throughout the anthology are original and new poems by Chrystos, Dylcia Pagan, Malkia M'Buzi Moore, Sarah Husein, Mary Jane Sullivan, Liz Roberts, and the late Marilyn Buck.

LOOK FOR ME IN THE WHIRLWIND
From the Panther 21 to 21st-Century Revolutions

Sekou Odinga, Dhoruba Bin Wahad, and Jamal Joseph
Edited by Matt Meyer & déqui kioni-sadiki
Foreword by Imam Jamil Al-Amin
Afterword by Mumia Abu-Jamal

$26.95
ISBN: 978-1-62963-389-3
6x9 • 648 pages

Amid music festivals and moon landings, the tumultuous year of 1969 included an infamous case in the annals of criminal justice and Black liberation: the New York City Black Panther 21. Though some among the group had hardly even met one another, the 21 were rounded up by the FBI and New York Police Department in an attempt to disrupt and destroy the organization that was attracting young people around the world. Involving charges of conspiracy to commit violent acts, the Panther 21 trial—the longest and most expensive in New York history—revealed the illegal government activities which led to exile, imprisonment on false charges, and assassination of Black liberation leaders. Solidarity for the 21 also extended well beyond "movement" circles and included mainstream publication of their collective autobiography, *Look for Me in the Whirlwind*.

Look for Me in the Whirlwind: From the Panther 21 to 21st-Century Revolutions contains the original and includes new commentary from surviving members of the 21. Still-imprisoned Sundiata Acoli, Imam Jamil Al-Amin, and Mumia Abu-Jamal contribute new essays. Never or rarely seen poetry and prose from Afeni Shakur, Kuwasi Balagoon, Ali Bey Hassan, and Michael "Cetewayo" Tabor is included. Early Panther leader and jazz master Bilal Sunni-Ali adds a historical essay and lyrics from his composition "Look for Me in the Whirlwind," and coeditors kioni-sadiki, Meyer, and Panther rank-and-file member Cyril "Bullwhip" Innis Jr. help bring the story up to date.

At a moment when the Movement for Black Lives recites the affirmation that "it is our duty to win," penned by Black Liberation Army (BLA) militant Assata Shakur, those who made up the BLA and worked alongside of Assata are largely unknown. This book provides essential parts of a hidden and missing-in-action history. Going well beyond the familiar and mythologized nostalgic Panther narrative, From the Panther 21 to 21st-Century Revolutions explains how and why the Panther legacy is still relevant and vital today.

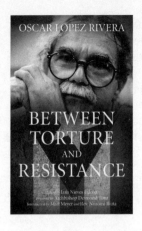

Oscar Lopez Rivera
Between Torture and Resistance
Oscar López Rivera
Edited by Luis Nieves Falcón
Foreword by Archbishop Desmond Tutu
Introduction by Matt Meyer
$18.00
ISBN: 978-1-60486-685-8
5.5x8.5 • 160 pages

The story of Puerto Rican leader Oscar López Rivera is one of courage, valor, and sacrifice. A decorated Viet Nam veteran and well-respected community activist, López Rivera now holds the distinction of being one of the longest held political prisoners in the world. Behind bars since 1981, López Rivera was convicted of the thought-crime of "seditious conspiracy," and never accused of causing anyone harm or of taking a life. This book is a unique introduction to his story and struggle, based on letters between him and the renowned lawyer, sociologist, educator, and activist Luis Nieves Falcón.

In photographs, reproductions of his paintings, and graphic content, Oscar's life is made strikingly accessible—so all can understand why this man has been deemed dangerous to the U.S. government. His ongoing fight for freedom, for his people and for himself (his release date is 2027, when he will be 84 years old), is detailed in chapters which share the life of a Latino child growing up in the small towns of Puerto Rico and the big cities of the U.S. It tells of his emergence as a community activist, of his life underground, and of his years in prison. Most importantly, it points the way forward.

With a vivid assessment of the ongoing colonial relationship between the U.S. and Puerto Rico, it provides tools for working for López Rivera's release— an essential ingredient if U.S.-Latin American relations, both domestically and internationally, have any chance of improvement. *Between Torture and Resistance* tells a sad tale of human rights abuses in the U.S. which are largely unreported. But it is also a story of hope—that there is beauty and strength in resistance.

> "In spite of the fact that here the silence from outside is more painful than the solitude inside the cave, the song of a bird or the sound of a cicada always reaches me to awaken my faith and keep me going."
> —Oscar López Rivera

LET FREEDOM RING
A Collection of Documents from the
Movements to Free U.S. Political
Prisoners
Edited by Matt Meyer
Foreword by Nobel Peace Laureate
Adolfo Perez Esquivel
Afterwords by Ashanti Alston and
Lynne Stewart
$37.95
ISBN: 978-1-60486-035-1
6x9 • 912 pages

Let Freedom Ring presents a two-decade sweep of essays, analyses, histories, interviews, resolutions, People's Tribunal verdicts, and poems by and about the scores of U.S. political prisoners and the campaigns to safeguard their rights and secure their freedom. In addition to an extensive section on the campaign to free death-row journalist Mumia Abu-Jamal, represented here are the radical movements that have most challenged the U.S. empire from within: Black Panthers and other Black liberation fighters, Puerto Rican independentistas, Indigenous sovereignty activists, white anti-imperialists, environmental and animal rights militants, Arab and Muslim activists, Iraq war resisters, and others. Contributors in and out of prison detail the repressive methods—from long-term isolation to sensory deprivation to politically inspired parole denial—used to attack these freedom fighters, some still caged after 30+ years. This invaluable resource guide offers inspiring stories of the creative, and sometimes winning, strategies to bring them home.

Contributors include: Mumia Abu-Jamal, Dan Berger, Dhoruba Bin-Wahad, Bob Lederer, Terry Bisson, Laura Whitehorn, Safiya Bukhari, The San Francisco 8, Angela Davis, Bo Brown, Bill Dunne, Jalil Muntaqim, Susie Day, Luis Nieves Falcón, Ninotchka Rosca, Meg Starr, Assata Shakur, Jill Soffiyah Elijah, Jan Susler, Chrystos, Jose Lopez, Leonard Peltier, Marilyn Buck, Oscar López Rivera, Sundiata Acoli, Ramona Africa, Linda Thurston, Desmond Tutu, Mairead Corrigan Maguire, and many more.

> "Within every society there are people who, at great personal risk and sacrifice, stand up and fight for the most marginalized among us. We call these people of courage, spirit and love, our heroes and heroines. This book is the story of the ones in our midst. It is the story of the best we are."
> —asha bandele, poet and author of *The Prisoner's Wife*

MAROON THE IMPLACABLE
The Collected Writings of Russell Maroon Shoatz
Russell Maroon Shoatz
Edited by Fred Ho and Quincy Saul
Foreword by Chuck D
Afterword by Matt Meyer and Nozizwe Madlala-Routledge
$20.00
ISBN: 978-1-60486-059-7
6x9 • 312 pages

Russell Maroon Shoatz is a political prisoner who has been held unjustly for over thirty years, including two decades in solitary confinement. He was active as a leader in the Black Liberation Movement in Philadelphia, both above and underground. His successful escapes from maximum-security prisons earned him the title "Maroon." This is the first published collection of his accumulated written works, and also includes new essays written expressly for this volume.

Despite the torture and deprivation that has been everyday life for Maroon over the last several decades, he has remained at the cutting edge of history through his writings. His work is innovative and revolutionary on multiple levels:

- His self-critical and fresh retelling of the Black liberation struggle in the U.S. includes many practical and theoretical insights;
- His analysis of the prison system, particularly in relation to capitalism, imperialism, and the drug war, takes us far beyond the recently-popular analysis of the Prison Industrial Complex, contained in books such as *The New Jim Crow*;
- His historical research and writings on Maroon communities throughout the Americas, drawing many insights from these societies in the fields of political and military revolutionary strategy are unprecedented; and finally
- His sharp and profound understanding of the current historical moment, with clear proposals for how to move forward embracing new political concepts and practices (including but not limited to eco-socialism, matriarchy and eco-feminism, food security, prefiguration, and the Occupy Wall Street movement) provide cutting-edge challenges for today's movements for social change.

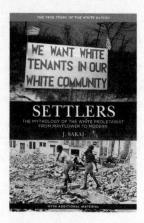

SETTLERS
The Mythology of the White Proletariat
from Mayflower to Modern
J. Sakai
$20.00
ISBN: 978-1-62963-037-3
6x9 • 456 pages

Settlers is a uniquely important book in the canon of the North American revolutionary left and anticolonial movements. First published in the 1980s by activists with decades of experience organizing in grassroots anticapitalist struggles against white supremacy, the book soon established itself as an essential reference point for revolutionary nationalists and dissident currents within the predominantly colonialist Marxist-Leninist and anarchist movements at that time.

Always controversial within the establishment Left *Settlers* uncovers centuries of collaboration between capitalism and white workers and their organizations, as well as their neocolonial allies, showing how the United States was designed from the ground up as a parasitic and genocidal entity. *Settlers* exposes the fact that America's white citizenry have never supported themselves but have always resorted to exploitation and theft, culminating in acts of genocide to maintain their culture and way of life. As recounted in painful detail by Sakai, the United States has been built on the theft of Indigenous lands and of Afrikan labor, on the robbery of the northern third of Mexico, the colonization of Puerto Rico, and the expropriation of the Asian working class, with each of these crimes being accompanied by violence.

This new edition includes "Cash & Genocide: The True Story of Japanese-American Reparations" and an interview with author J. Sakai by Ernesto Aguilar.

> "*Settlers* is a critical analysis of the colonization of the Americas that overturns the 'official' narrative of poor and dispossessed European settlers to reveal the true nature of genocidal invasion and land theft that has occurred for over five hundred years. If you want to understand the present, you must know the past, and this book is a vital contribution to that effort."
> —Gord Hill, author of *500 Years of Indigenous Resistance*

About
PM Press

politics • culture • art • fiction • music • film

PM Press was founded at the end of 2007 by a small collection of folks with decades of publishing, media, and organizing experience. PM Press co-conspirators have published and distributed hundreds of books, pamphlets, CDs, and DVDs. Members of PM have founded enduring book fairs, spearheaded victorious tenant organizing campaigns, and worked closely with bookstores, academic conferences, and even rock bands to deliver political and challenging ideas to all walks of life. We're old enough to know what we're doing and young enough to know what's at stake.

We seek to create radical and stimulating fiction and nonfiction books, pamphlets, T-shirts, visual and audio materials to entertain, educate, and inspire you. We aim to distribute these through every available channel with every available technology, whether that means you are seeing anarchist classics at our bookfair stalls; reading our latest vegan cookbook at the café; downloading geeky fiction e-books; or digging new music and timely videos from our website.

Contact us for direct ordering and questions about all PM Press releases, as well as manuscript submissions, review copy requests, foreign rights sales, author interviews, to book an author for an event, and to have PM Press attend your bookfair:

PM Press
PO Box 23912
Oakland CA 94623
510-658-3906

PM Press in Europe
europe@pmpress.org
www.pmpress.org.uk

Buy books and stay on top of what we are doing at:

www.pmpress.org

FOPM

These are indisputably momentous times—the financial system is melting down globally and the Empire is stumbling. Now more than ever there is a vital need for radical ideas.

In the many years since its founding—and on a mere shoestring—PM Press has risen to the formidable challenge of publishing and distributing knowledge and entertainment for the struggles ahead. With over 200 releases to date, we have published an impressive and stimulating array of literature, art, music, politics, and culture. Using every available medium, we've succeeded in connecting those hungry for ideas and information to those putting them into practice.

Friends of PM allows you to directly help impact, amplify, and revitalize the discourse and actions of radical writers, filmmakers, and artists. It provides us with a stable foundation from which we can build upon our early successes and provides a much-needed subsidy for the materials that can't necessarily pay their own way. You can help make that happen—and receive every new title automatically delivered to your door once a month—by joining as a Friend of PM Press. And, we'll throw in a free T-Shirt when you sign up.

Here are your options:
- $30 a month: Get all books and pamphlets plus 50% discount on all webstore purchases
- $40 a month: Get all PM Press releases (including CDs and DVDs) plus 50% discount on all webstore purchases
- $100 a month: Superstar—Everything plus PM merchandise, free downloads, and 50% discount on all webstore purchases

For those who can't afford $30 or more a month, we have *Sustainer Rates* at $15, $10 and $5. Sustainers get a free PM Press T-shirt and a 50% discount on all purchases from our website.

Your Visa or Mastercard will be billed once a month, until you tell us to stop. Or until our efforts succeed in bringing the revolution around. Or the financial meltdown of Capital makes plastic redundant. Whichever comes first.